Reader

"Every reader who wishes to hear from the Lord regarding a situation should read, *There Is A Word from the Lord*. Prophetess Stephanie Moore meticulously identifies situations. She gives a clear definition and pertinent message. The writing is clear and accessible so as to dispel any ambiguity about its message. The reader should experience a spiritual rejuvenation packed with encouragement. The encouragement promised for thirty-one days will extend into the reader's future, resulting in spiritual growth. I highly recommend *There Is A Word from the Lord* by Prophetess Stephanie Moore."
- Dr. Claudia Wells Hamilton

"WOW! What a Great Word from the Lord, I'm so glad she wrote this book telling a dying world that Jesus lives inside of us. I know the Trinity is favoring her life. Stephanie, just keep on living for Christ and others will see and know you are chosen by God; the one that is Alpha and Omega."
- Sophia M. Starks

"Prophetess Moore shares her gift with others through everyday words that help the reader understand, meditate, and succeed in life. The message is clearly delivered for readers in all walks of life. This book can serve as a guide through some of life's difficult journeys as well as daily living."
- Linda Selden, Retired Principal, Hampton City Schools

"Wow.....Such an inspirational text that is based solely on the Word of

God! Each installment (or day) provides practical teaching regarding what God's Word is saying to the Body of Christ. Prophetess Stephanie Moore's inspirational text is a must-read for anyone who desires to 'digest' God's Word and apply it to his or her life."
- Alexis E. Foster, Educator and Musician

"The excerpts from your book, *There Is A Word From The Lord*, were so amazing because of the special emphasis placed on important topics with extraordinary simplicity. God continues to show us His will and plan for our lives through this book. Thank you Mother Moore for being that instrument used by God to give us encouragement as we continue to fight a good fight of faith while it is yet day."
- Apostle Jimmy L. Joyner, Sr., Fellowship Apostle, Tower Of Deliverance Fellowship

"What a blessing to the Body of Christ and to all who are seeking a closer walk with our Blessed Savior. *There Is A Word From The Lord*, is clearly Prophetess Moore's unselfish way of sharing the treasured chest of golden nuggets that can only be attained through a personal intimate exhcange that has been solidified between her and her Lord. Flesh and blood alone certainly could not reveal these precious life lessons! So it is with great pride and anticipation that I endorse this power-packed volume of bible teaching and revelation. This is truly an outstanding gift that Prophetess Moore has submitted to the Saints in the form of a daily biblical study with practical application. What a blessing!"
- Janice Webster, Educator, Jacksonville Florida

There is a Word from the Lord

31 Days of Encouragement

Beloved
I wish above all things that
you would prosper and be in
health even as your soul prospers
I have wisdom that I long to
share with you to show you how to
succeed in every area of your life
But I need you to take seriously
what I tell you and incorporate the
wisdom into your daily practice

There is a Word from the Lord

31 Days of Encouragement

by

Prophetess Stephanie Moore

KINGDOM RULE
PUBLISHING
WWW.KINGDOMRULE.COM

A division of Consuming Fire Incorporated
WWW.CONSUMINGFIREINC.COM

ATLANTA, GEORGIA

Published by Kingdom Rule Publishing, a subsidiary of Consuming Fire Incorporated.

Kingdom Rule Nonfiction.

Kingdom Rule Publishing
8664 Thomas Rd., Riverdale, GA 30274

Kingdom Rule Publishing is a subsidiary of Consuming Fire Incorporated
Visit our website at www.consumingfireinc.com

Printed in the United States of America

First Kingdom Rule Publishing Printing: November 2013
ISBN: 978-1481959384

Cover design by Stephen Blackmon.

— FOREWORD —

$\mathscr{I}$ was walking in the morning, as was my usual custom that summer, and I was talking to God. I began to express my concerns with the LORD for the day regarding my current transportation situation. My car had broken down one day and the LORD was dealing with me as I walked down the street. HE told me to go to the dealership between two and two thirty the next day. That night I asked the LORD what to put on the license plate. He said, "God's favor." When I walked into the dealership, I said, "My credit is bad and I have been bankrupt and I just believe GOD for a car." The salesman told me to go and pick out what I wanted.

I was excited to watch God work on my behalf. The gentleman told me to write a check for $500; however, it would not be deposited until the end of the month. I said "Beautiful" because I did not have any income. I was so excited because I had driven off the lot in a 2000 Ford Contour and it was the summer of 2002. God had delivered just as He said He would. Time passed and the end of the month drew near, I still had no income, but I was trusting God. I said, "LORD, now what am I going to do?" The LORD said to call back and make arrangements, and the dealership accepted the new arrangements, and I went down the road with my car.

In 2007, I met Apostle Gene W. Boyd of Tower of Deliverance Fellowship. I shared my vision with him of what the LORD told me: that I would be on the radio and television, and that I would write books. In December, just before the New Year, he informed me that Tower of Deliverance and E and E Enterprises would sponsor me on the radio. I was taken back by this information. I had no idea that God was going to use this fellowship to open up these doors. I had been to so many places and had so many experiences with churches that focused on tearing me down and stripping the very visions and dreams from me that I was amazed to find myself in a place of encouragement.

Apostle Boyd informed me that I would be on the radio the first Monday in January 2008. They asked me what is going to be the name of your radio broadcast. I looked at my license plate and said G-favor and then said there is a word from the LORD because God has always dealt with me with just one word. And He would give me the scriptures to expound on that word. This is how G-favor truly began and the book provides written documentation of 31 days of my radio broadcast. And so the journey begins each day with just one word from the LORD.

– DEDICATION –

This book is dedicated to the loving memory of my mother, Pearlie Estella Daniels. My mother was a faith walker without truly realizing what that would ever mean to me. When growing up, I witnessed how my mother would say what she wanted and each and every time, she got it. I remember one particular incident that was truly amazing and inspiring to any who heard of it. My mother purchased a car without even knowing the slightest thing about how to drive it. She explained to me that she was tired of asking people for a ride here and there. So, she bought her own car with no license and no information on how to drive a car whatsoever. However, she learned how to drive and got her license.

When I accepted Christ in my life, my first Pastor, Bishop Samuel L. Green Jr. taught on faith, and I finally grasped that concept. It was during that time that I made a full connection to the teachings of the word of God, and what I witnessed my mother do throughout my whole life. After Bishop Green's teaching, I began my journey as a faith walker.

– ACKNOWLEDGEMENTS –

$\mathscr{I}$thank God for supplying me with His words and for ordering my steps. I give God all of the glory the honor and the praise for all He has done in my life. I also thank God for every individual He brought to provide me with words of encouragement and inspiration while I was writing this book. I especially thank God for Apostle Gene W. Boyd and Apostle Ernest Green of Tower of Deliverance Fellowship (TODF), who played a major role in the writing of this book. TODF, along with E&E Enterprises, were the ones who sponsored G-Favor Ministries Radio Broadcast in the beginning of this journey, and I am eternally grateful for that. I am extremely grateful for all the support I have received from Mother Carol Boyd and Mother Marie Green. I also thank God for Apostle Jimmy and Mother Delores Joyner, Apostle Kenneth Howard and Mother Vanita Howard for their continuous encouragement and Pastor and Mrs. Audley Lewis as well for their continued support of my radio ministry.

I would especially like to thank Professor Lakenhia

Gould, whom I consider to be my spiritual daughter. For she has been my backbone throughout this process. She has edited and helped me express these experiences. She has encouraged and helped me in so many different ways. I would also like to thank Brenda Morst, who gave me the information concerning this great publisher. My darling daughter, Darlisha, who is always near and dear to my heart and her daughters Amorae and Assani; they all serve as a continuous source of inspiration. My beloved son Pastor John A. Moore, III, the most faithful and caring son a mother could have, and his lovely wife Kenya Moore, who fill my heart with great joy; they are always in my corner.

Pastor Vanessa Hinton, my dear friend, assisted me in many ways. She kept me focused by ensuring that our conversations were few and far between during this project, and I thank her for that. I was also inspired by my sister Marvinia Owens and my brothers: the late Antonio Daniels, Marvin Lee Daniels Jr., Dwight Daniels, Lorenzo Saboor, and the late Gregory Daniels. I would also like to take this time to express my thanks for my father, the late Marvin Lee Daniels, Sr., and my late mother Pearlie Estella Daniels. I would also like to thank my Aunt Eva Parson, my cousins: Janice Williams and Preston Butler for their continued support over the years.

I extend a most sincere thanks to Pastor Adrienne Brooks for inspiring me and keeping me energized. I thank God for my niece Wanda Wilson, who helped me with my computer needs, my niece Attorney Tamena Wilson, who helped me with my legal needs, and all my other cousins, nieces and nephews. Pam Cook, my former co-worker told me at the beginning of G-favor Ministries to just be myself and talk to the people. I am eternally grateful to Pam Cook for these words, for they gave me the confidence I needed in the beginning to go forward and do God's will. I extend a heartfelt thanks to the Moffett family; especially Teresa Moffett, who was an inspiration. I want to thank Tammy Davis, who sang on the broadcast to the glory of God, Dorothy Harris, and her daughter Cynthia Palmer, who have always supported me in all my endeavors.

— CONTENTS —

There is a Word from the Lord

31 Days of Encouragement

Beloved I wish above all things that you should prosper and be in health even as your soul prospers. I have wisdom that I long to share with you to show you how to succeed in every area of your life. But I need you to take seriously what I tell you and incorporate the wisdom into your daily practice.

Day 1:

TODAY'S SCRIPTURES:
Deuteronomy 31:12-13
Psalm 4:1
Psalm 51:8
Psalm85:8
Luke 16:31
John 5:25
John 12:47
Roman 10:14
James 1:19

Hear

Definition of Hear

To perceive by the ear; to apprehend or take cognizance of by the ear; as, to hear sounds; to hear a voice; to hear one call.

Deuteronomy 31:12-13

"Gather the people together, men and women, and children, and thy stranger that is within thy gates, that they may hear, and that they may learn, and fear the LORD your God, and observe to do all the words of this law: And that their children, which have not known any thing, may hear, and learn to fear the LORD your God, as long as ye live in the land whither ye go over Jordan to possess it."

21

THERE IS A WORD FROM THE LORD

Message

My friend, in these scriptures, the priests were given the responsibility of reading the laws and instructing the people: men, women, the little ones, and the strangers). The word of God was for all to hear. My dear friend, we as people of God and leaders have the responsibility to teach and preach the word of God.

Psalm 4:1

"Hear me when I call, O God of my righteousness: thou hast enlarged me when I was in distress; have mercy upon me, and hear my prayer."

Message

My friend, in this scripture, the pressing psalmist is facing a very real need, but his confidence in God remains especially strong. He addresses God in terms of His character and His righteousness. Then he speaks of God's earlier works in his life, when God saved David: You have relieved me in my distress. Friend, find peace in God's presence, despite the circumstance or situation. Even when torn by physical and emotional pain, a person may still have restful sleep.

Psalm 51:8

"Make me to hear joy and gladness; that the bones which thou hast broken may rejoice."

<u>Message</u>

My friend, in this psalm King David knew there was ultimately only one way to deal with sin; face it, confess, and be forgiven. The sins that he committed were adultery with Bathsheba, the wife of Uriah and engineering Uriah's death when he discovered Bathsheba had become pregnant. David repeatedly called for his cleansing. In this psalm, he expressed his profound sense of guilt. David was asking that his heart be renewed, restored and transformed. My friend, God is the only source of such a renewal.

Psalm 85:8

"I will hear what God the LORD will speak: for he will speak peace unto his people and to his saints: but let them not turn again to folly."

<u>Message</u>

My friend, in this scripture, the psalmist is expecting to hear a direct revelation from the LORD. Such a revelation would be consistent with God's character. Peace suggests wholeness; fullness; things, as they ought to be. The word saint is related to the term translated mercy these are people who reflect the love of God in their own lives, and they do not turn back to folly or foolishness. My friend, God's blessing will continue only as long as the people remain faithful to Him. His salvation can be described as any act of mercy on the part of God.

Luke 16:31

"And he said unto him, If they hear not Moses and the prophets, neither will they be persuaded, though one rose from the dead."

Message

My friend, if they reject God's message, they will not be persuaded by the resurrection; they have to have ears to hear. Though the rich man's request for a heavenly messenger is denied within the parable, it is honored in the telling of the account because the parable is part of a gospel that announces Christ's resurrection. My friend, I am so glad that I accepted the resurrection of Christ over thirty some years ago. My life has not been the same.

John 5:25

"Verily, verily, I say unto you, The hour is coming, and now is, when the dead shall hear the voice of the Son of God: and they that hear shall live."

Message

My friend, now is in the present. Christ gives spiritual life to the spiritually dead. My friend, if you know that you are not able to hear the voice of Christ while you are living, you know that you will not be able to hear it when you die.

John 12:47

"And if any man hear my words, and believe not, I judge him not: for I came not to judge the world, but to save the world."

Message

My friend, as John stated, we are not here to execute judgment. Christ will judge, but at His first coming, He did not come to judge but to save. My friend Jesus has come to save us, to deliver us from sin.

Romans 10:14

"How then shall they call on him in whom they have not believed? and how shall they believe in him of whom they have not heard? and how shall they hear without a preacher?"

Message

My friend, if salvation is to be made possible for everyone, God must send preachers; so, that people can hear and believe. My friend, a preacher is not just someone talking while in the pulpit, but someone who is willing to share the gospel—one who has truly been born again and has had the experiences of being born again.

James 1:19

"Wherefore, my beloved brethren, let every man be swift to hear, slow to speak, slow to wrath:"

<u>Message</u>

My friend, enduring trials lead to a crown of life and yielding to temptation can lead to physical death. Therefore, the believer in the midst of a trial needs to be swift to hear, slow to speak, and slow to wrath. If a believer gets angry in difficult circumstances, the practical righteousness of God will not be evident in his or her life. When someone does wrong to us, the natural reaction is to retaliate. Most of the time, this retaliation is verbally, but this response does not glorify God. Holding one's tongue, trying to understand the other person's position, and leaving vengeance to God demonstrates Godly love.

Day 2:

TODAY'S SCRIPTURES:
Exodus 19:9
II Chronicles 20:20
Mark 5:35-36
Mark 9:23
Mark 11:24
John 14:1
Roman 10:9
II Corinthians 4:12-13
Hebrew 11:6

Believe

Definition of Believe

To credit upon the authority or testimony of another; to be persuaded of the truth of, upon evidence furnished by reasons, arguments, and deductions of the mind, or by circumstances other than personal knowledge; to regard or accept as true; to place confidence in; to think; to consider; as, to believe a person, a statement, or a doctrine.

Exodus 19:9

"And the LORD said unto Moses, Lo, I come unto thee in a thick cloud, that the people may hear when I speak with thee, and believe thee forever. And Moses told the words of the

27

people unto the LORD."

Message

My friend, God was able to reveal only so much of His splendor to a people who were unprepared for a full revelation. He appeared to them in the thick cloud, His elusive presence. The omnipotent creator came down to meet the Israelites. His presence evoked an overwhelming sense of awe. Later in the same chapter of Exodus, verses 18-19, the LORD descended upon Mount Sinai. The entire mountain was smoking and the LORD came in fire. The smoke was an enveloping cover for the glory of the LORD, even as the associated fire further reinforced God's presence to the Israelites. These visitations served to reinforce their belief in the LORD. My friend, even today we are blessed by how the LORD visits us through His Holy Spirit.

II Chronicles 20:20

"And they rose early in the morning, and went forth into the wilderness of Tekoa: and as they went forth, Jehoshaphat stood and said, Hear me, O Judah, and ye inhabitants of Jerusalem; Believe in the LORD your God, so shall ye be established; believe his prophets, so shall ye prosper."

Message

My friend, when the Moabites and Amorites, who were the descendents of Lot by his two daughters, came against Israel, King Jehoshaphat needed a plan of action. He picked one. Jehoshaphat prayed and believed God. God answered his prayer. Israel won the battle and prospered. When Jehoshaphat and his people came to take away the spoils; they found among them in abundance both riches with the dead bodies and precious jewels, which they stripped off for themselves more than they could carry away. There was so much that they were gathering those spoils for three days. God blessed them because they believed the prophet.

Mark 5:35-36

"While he yet spake, there came from the ruler of the synagogue's house certain which said, Thy daughter is dead: why troublest thou the Master any further? As soon as Jesus heard the word that was spoken, he saith unto the ruler of the synagogue, Be not afraid only believe."

Message

My friend, the implications of the girl's reported death is that her condition is now irreversible and without remedy. Jesus immediately corrects this thought by insisting that Jarius stops being afraid and continues to believe that there is yet hope for her. When the girl rose, this indicated that her life had been restored, just as in the case of the widow's dead son in Luke 7:15 and of Lazarus who had been dead for four days in John 11:39. All three will die again. Jesus' resurrection, however, was unique. Not only was He restored to life, but Jesus' body was transformed so that He would never have to face death again. God is good!

Mark 9:23

"Jesus said unto him, 'If thou canst believe, all things are possible to him that believeth.'"

<u>Message</u>

My friend, all things are possible because Jesus healed the child from the dumb and deaf spirit. My dear friend, although a grain of faith is sufficient—a person's faith needs to grow and mature. One can only receive as much as he or she believes. God will supply our basic needs, not because we try harder, but because we believe him more. I can remember one of the first times I really operated in faith. I was single, and I wanted to move to the peninsula (a different part of Hampton Roads, Virginia from where I was staying). I shared my desires with the LORD. The LORD gave me favor, and I got an apartment and I didn't even have a job. Someone paid the first month's rent. I needed to pay the next month's rent. I went to the supermarket to talk to the manager and shared with him that I needed a job and told him he could not find anyone better than me for this job. God gave me favor, and I got the job. I have been a faith walker every since that experience.

Mark 11:24

"Therefore, I say unto you, What things so ever ye desire, when ye pray, believe that ye receive them, and ye shall have them."

Message

My friend, the key to prayer is to believe. However, there are other factors that do apply. All things must be "According to His will", and it has to be in Jesus' name. What makes believing so powerful is when we stand on that belief until we see the manifestation or our faith, but we must believe it before we receive it or all is lost.

John 14:1

"Let not your heart be troubled: ye believe in God, believe also in me."

Message

My friend, after announcing Judas' betrayal, His own imminent departure, and Peter's denial, Jesus told His disciples not to be troubled but to trust Him. Believe. Believe, the simple but profound solution to all our problems is believing. My friend, we do what we do because we believe what we are doing is right. Our actions are nothing more than the product of our deepest convictions. The key to this belief and the source of it is our faith. Right thinking is essential to engage in the right action and right thinking begins with thinking right about God.

Romans 10:9

"That if thou shalt confess with thy mouth the LORD Jesus, and shalt believe in thine heart that God hath raised Him from the dead, thou shalt be saved."

Message

My friend, confess; come before the LORD, believe what is said in this verse. Once the heart is right, all one has to do is repent, believe in Jesus, and confess that belief.

II Corinthians 4:12-13

"So then death worketh in us, but life in you. We having the same spirit of faith, according as it is written, I believed, and therefore have I spoken; we also believe, and therefore speak;"

Message

Had Paul not been willing to risk death to bring the gospel to Corinth, the Corinthians would not have received eternal life. Paul explains why he was willing to risk his life for the gospel. His belief in the gospel compelled him to tell others about the resurrection of Jesus Christ. My friend, are you risking your life to tell others about Jesus Christ? Paul's belief was focused on the God of resurrection; the evidence of God's power motivated him to face difficulties, danger, and death for Christ's sake. My friend, as Paul rested in what he knew about God, not what he felt, we too must rest in God and boldly do His will.

Hebrews 11:6

"But without faith it is impossible to please him: for, he that cometh to God must believe that he is, and that he is a rewarder of them that diligently seek him."

<u>Message</u>

Here, the author of Hebrews explains that faith is mandatory for those who approach God. God rewards not only those who seek Him, but those who do good works in the power of the Holy Spirit. Christ's rewards are meant to provide a powerful incentive for an obedient life.

Day 3:

TODAY'S SCRIPTURES:
Job 14:14
Psalms 27:14
Psalms 62:5
Isaiah 40:31
Lamentations 3:26

Wait

Definition of Wait

To stay or rest in expectation; to stop or remain stationary till the arrival of some person or event; to rest in patience; to stay; not to depart.

Job 14:14

"If a man die, shall he live again? All the days of my appointed time will I wait, till my change come."

Message

Job's question 'if a man dies, shall he live again' is answered with an emphatic yes by Jesus in the New Testament. But Job responds to his own question with a determination

35

to wait for his change to come. Since Job considers life hard, (7:1). Perhaps he is implying that he will wait for relief from his suffering through death to find out the answer. My friend, when you continue to read the account about Job, you find that God delivered Job from his afflictions and blessed him more than double for his troubles. My friend, if you just wait on God, He will bring you out.

Psalms 27:14

"Wait on the LORD: be of good courage, and he shall strengthen thine heart: wait, I say, on the LORD."

<u>Message</u>

My friend, to wait on the LORD is to demonstrate confidence and an expectation for HIM to work on your behalf. The Hebrew word for wait may also be translated "hope." To hope in God is to wait for His timing and His action. Life is not really about us at all. It's about Jesus being glorified in our lives, and our becoming witnesses for Him. So, wait on Jesus and remember the scripture Romans 8:28 while you wait. "And we know all things work together for the good to them that love God, to them who are the called according to his purpose." God is working it out.

Psalms 62:5

"My soul, wait thou only upon God; for my expectation is from him."

Message

My friend, while waiting on the LORD, remember that He loves you and cares about you. I often think about going to a doctor's appointment whenever the LORD tells us to wait. . When you go for that doctor's appointment, sometimes you have to wait for 30-45 minutes, but eventually that doctor comes out to see you. He lets you know what your problem is and gives you some direction concerning how to fix your problem. Waiting on the LORD is also like waiting at a bus stop; the bus is going to come and take you to where you need to go. My friend, just wait on the LORD, He is going to answer your prayers and bring you victories like no other.

Isaiah 40:31

"But they that wait upon the LORD shall renew their strength; they shall mount up with wings as eagles; they shall run, and not be weary; and they shall walk, and not faint."

Message

To wait entails confidence and expectation and active hope in the LORD. The LORD gives power to those who trust in Him. Hope is not a wishful thought, but a confident expectation in the LORD.

Lamentations 3:25

"The LORD is good unto them that wait for him, to the soul

that seeketh him."

Message

My friend, those who wait on the LORD are those who have accepted God's will and timing.

Day 4:

TODAY'S SCRIPTURES:
Isaiah 51:1
Hosea 6:3
Matthew 4:19
John 12:26
I Timothy 6:11
III John 11

Follow

Definition of Follow

To go or come after, go along as in accompany, pursue, obey, keep the eyes or attention on, keep up with and understand, be concern with, go or come after someone or something else.

Isaiah 51:1

"Hearken to me, ye that follow after righteousness, ye that seek the LORD: look unto the rock whence ye are hewn, and to the hole of the pit whence ye are digged."

Message

My friend, as you continue to read this passage of the

39

scriptures, you'll see that God is telling His people to follow the pattern of Abraham—trust God. We are living in a time when you really have to know God for yourself and trust Him. There are many winds of doctrines trying to tell you which way you should go, but you have to know where God is leading you. You have to be honest with yourself and follow God and obey Him. If you have doubts or concerns, you must address them and not just pretend they don't exist. There is nothing wrong with asking God to help your weakest times, especially when you are tryng to follow Him. Listen to His instruction and stay in the habit of listening and obeying, it can't be something that is done just some of the time.

Hosea 6:3

"Then shall we know, if we follow on to know the LORD: his going forth is prepared as the morning; and he shall come unto us as the rain, as the latter and former rain unto the earth."

Message

My friend, the word follow is for the people of God. When God's people truly repent, God is right there to restore His relationship with them. God's restored presence in us automatically provides us with His blessings. These blessings will be like rain that waters and renews the earth; so shall we, who were once dead in sin be renewed. The latter rain refers to the rain in the spring that causes the plants to grow; the former rains came in the autumn and softened the ground for plowing and sowing. So my friend, that is how God is going to pour His blessing upon His people. When we follow after Him, we will reap a great harvest. The blessing will come and over take you. Follow the Lord Jesus Christ!

Matthew 4:19

"And he saith unto them, Follow me, and I will make you fishers of men."

Message

My friend, when I read this scripture, it was so encouraging. God delights in using ordinary, insignificant people. God has no respect of persons. God will use whomsoever He will. Lessons learned in everyday life and while working will prove valuable in serving Christ. The fishermen could use their experience in netting people for the Lord.

John 12:26

"If any man serve me, let him follow me; and where I am, there shall also my servant be: if any man serve me, him will my Father honour."

Message

Follow me in this context means to follow Jesus' example, his personal sacrifice. My friend, Jesus set the example by abandoning his life to save the lives of others and fulfill his destiny.

I Timothy 6:11

"But thou, O man of God, flee these things; and follow after righteousness, godliness, faith, love, patience, meekness."

<u>Message</u>

My friend, don't follow after the ungodly things in life, but rather follow after the characteristics outlined for righteous men and women: righteousness, godliness, faith, love, patience, and gentleness. These traits are the fruit of the spirit, which provide the children of God with a peace that surpasses all understanding. Men and women of God should pursue godliness, not materialism, with all of their being.

III John 11:1

"Beloved, follow not that which is evil, but that which is good. He that doeth good is of God: but he that doeth evil hath not seen God."

<u>Message</u>

My friend, the proof of our commitment to God is that we personally reject evil and embrace a life patterned after that which is good. The lifestyle that we exhibit is a direct reflection of the extent to which we have seen and embraced God. If we were to see God perfectly, we would never sin; our sin is a result of a faulty vision of God. Therefore, the scriptures encourage us to look at Christ; for the day when we see Him perfectly, will be the day that we will be like Him.

Day 5:

TODAY'S SCRIPTURES:
Numbers 12:6
Job 33:15-16
Psalms 126:6
Matthew 2:12
Matthew 27:19
Acts 2:17

Dreams

Definition of Dreams
Images passing through the mind during sleep, something having great beauty or charm.

Numbers 12:6

"And he said, Hear now my words: If there be a prophet among you, I the LORD will make myself known unto him in a vision, and will speak unto him in a dream."

<u>Message</u>

My friend, the language used there conveyed that God was in control. He spoke to whomever He wished and in the manner of His choosing. God is a spirit. Moses had an intimate relationship with God; he almost spoke to him face to face. As you continue to read this discourse you discover that God dealt with Aaron and Miriam for talking against Moses because he married an Ethiopian. When God speaks to you, others can't hear what He said to you; therefore, when you go forward in what He has told you to do, they think it's not God. But my friend, you have to learn to obey God regardless of what people think or say. God will vindicate you. God will justify you.

Job 33:15-16

"In a dream, in a vision of the night, when deep sleep falleth upon men, in slumberings upon the bed; Then he openeth the ears of men, and sealeth their instruction."

Message

When Job complained of nightmares, Elihu suggested that God may have been trying to teach Job something through a dream or vision of the night. My friend, sometimes God will reveal things to us through dreams and visions. Don't take it lightly, just observe and see what happens.

Psalms 126:1

"When the LORD turned again the captivity of Zion, we were like them that dream."

<u>Message</u>

When the children of Israel returned from Babylonian captivity, it was a moment they anticipated for so long, it seemed like a dream. Some of the Israelites had waited a lifetime. The joy of the Israelites could not be contained; their praise to God was unstoppable. Sometimes in your life, when you've been waiting a long time for something to happen, when it does happen, it is like a dream—you can hardly believe it. That's how it was for the children of Israel, and so will it be for you and I .God is about to do something for you and I that is going to seem like a dream, but my friend it is going to be a reality.

<u>Matthew 2:12</u>

"And being warned of God in a dream that they should not return to Herod they departed into their own Country another way."

<u>Message</u>

My friend, dreams of divine guidance emphasize that not only is God watching over you, but He will direct you out of harm's way. It is up to you to obey what God reveals to you. You never know what dangers lay ahead, but God sees and knows everything, let Him direct your path.

<u>Matthew 27:19</u>

"When he was set down on the judgment seat, his wife sent

unto him saying, Have thou nothing to do with that just man: for I have suffered many things this day in a dream because of him."

Message

My friend, only Matthew records this incident concerning Pilate's wife. It highlights Pilate's sense of responsibility; he did not want to condemn an innocent man. Barabbas was notorious; he was an insurrectionist and a murderer. Pilate assumed the Jews would release Jesus over a murderer like Barabbas. Jesus had only done good, never evil. Pilate pronounced Jesus to be innocent. The washing of his hands is recorded only by Matthew. Pilate vainly attempted to rid himself of the guilt attached to condemning the "just man" to death. The Jews proudly said Jesus' blood would be on them and their children. My friend, the destruction of Jerusalem was one of the results of this sin.

Acts 2:17

"And it shall come to pass in the last days saith God, I will pour out of my Spirit upon all flesh; and your sons and your daughters shall prophecy, and your young men shall see visions, and your old men shall dream dreams."

Message

Peter began his sermon on the Day of Pentecost by quoting Joel 2:28-32. God promised that there would be a time

PROPHETESS STEPHANIE MOORE

when all those who followed Him would receive His spirit, not just prophets, kings and priests. My friend, God would speak to and through all those who would come to Him, whether in visions, dreams, or prophecy. This is the beginning of the last days. God's final act of salvation began with the pouring out of HIS Spirit. The final act of deliverance will continue to the end of this age. Remember that Joel prophesied that the spirit would come. Jesus fulfilled that promise when He sent the Spirit. My friend, Jesus is not dead. He could not send the Spirit, if He was dead. He ascended to heaven and sits at the right hand of God, the Father Almighty.

Day 6:

Deuteronomy 33:27
John 3:15-16
John 5:39
Roman 6:23
II Corinthians 4:18
II Corinthians 5:1
Hebrews 6:1-2

Eternal

Definition of Eternal
All of time, all the past and all the future, time without beginning or ending, the endless period after death.

Deuteronomy 33:27

"The eternal God is thy refuge, and underneath are the everlasting arms: and he shall thrust out the enemy from before thee: and shall say, Destroy them."

Message

My friend, the LORD continually equips His children to defend themselves against the attacks of the enemy. Our Divine Warrior is always providing protection, He never

49

sleeps. God is a refuge and a fortress for the people to flee to in times of distress. The God who redeemed Israel with His strong arm will always be with His people, which was made evident by His love and His power. My friend, today we as Christians serve that same God that the Hebrews served. We serve Him through His Son Jesus Christ.

John 3:15-16

"That whosoever believeth in him should not perish, but have eternal life. For God so loved the world that he gave his only begotten Son, that whosoever believeth in him should not perish, but have everlasting life."

<u>Message</u>

When a person accepts Christ, he or she is born again and receives eternal life, a spiritual one. One learns to live the way God would have him or her to live. It must be His way, not ours. My friend, the focus is not on our faith, but on Christ, the foundation of our faith. Faith doesn't save. It is the channel to the one who saves—Jesus. God so loved the world, He gave up His one and only to offer salvation. God's love is not restricted to any one nation or to any spiritually elite group. "The world" includes all creations.

John 5:39

"Search the scriptures for in them ye think ye have eternal life: and they are they which testify of me."

<u>Message</u>

My friend, the Jewish Religious Leaders of Jesus' day diligently searched the Old Testament scriptures. However, they did not believe Jesus was the Messiah. Therefore, they did not believe in him. There are also those today who master the scriptures, but do not allow the scriptures to have a place in their heart. My friend, people do not have difficulty finding evidence today, they suffer from a lack of willingness to accept the truth when presented, which would bring them to Christ. In 2 Thessalonians 2:10, it says, "And with all deceivableness of unrighteousness in them that perish; because they received not the love of the truth, that they might be saved." People make a conscious choice to reject Christ and God's love.

Romans 6:23

"For the wages of sin is death; but the gift of God is eternal life through Jesus Christ our LORD"

<u>Message</u>

My friend, sin results in death, but God gives the gift of eternal life. By walking in faith and obedience, Christians are able to fully enjoy God's free gift of eternal life.

II Corinthians 4:18

"While we look not at the things which are seen, but at the things which are not seen: for the things which are seen are temporal; but the things which are not seen are eternal."

Message

My friend, in order to not lose hope, the believer needs to shift his or her focus from that which is seen to that which is not seen; from temporary problems to the glorious eternal rewards he or she will receive.

II Corinthians 5:1

"For we know that if our earthly house of this tabernacle were dissolved, we have a building of God, an house not made with hands, eternal in the heavens."

Message

My friend, the human body is like a house, which is easily dismantled and demolished; it will be destroyed unless death is preceded by the rapture. The believer's future house, his resurrected body, is a building made by God in a structure established for eternity.

Hebrews 6:1-2

"Therefore leaving the principles of the doctrine of Christ let us go unto perfection, not laying again the foundation of repentance from dead works and of faith toward God. Of the doctrine of baptisms and of laying on of hands and of resurrection of the dead, and of eternal judgment."

<u>Message</u>

My friend Paul is telling us to leave the basics and go on to perfection, meaning maturity. Eternal judgment refers to the belief that everyone will be judged by the great Judge. The scriptures indicate that there are two judgments: one for believers, in which Jesus determines every believer's reward, the other judgment is for nonbelievers and it is one of condemnation.

Day 7:

Fatherless

TODAY'S SCRIPTURES:
Psalms 10:14
Psalms 146:9
Proverb 23:10
James 1:27

Definition of Fatherless
Without having a father in one's life, living without a father.

Psalms 10:14

"Thou hast seen it for thou beholdest mischief and spite, to requite it with the hand: the poor committeth himself unto thee; thou art the helper of the fatherless."

Message

My friend, you have seen the classic confession of trust in God in the psalms of lament. God does know, He does see and He will act. God protects those like the fatherless who

55

have no other protection.

Psalms 146:9

"The LORD preserveth the strangers; He relieveth the fatherless and widow but the way of the wicked He turneth upside down."

Message

My friend, God is gracious to the fatherless, the helpless, the lonely and the needy. God is helping you now, even unbeknownst to you.

Proverb 23:10

"Remove not the old land mark; and enter not into the fields of the fatherless."

Message

My friend, the tendency of evil people in all ages is to take advantage of the helpless. But the destroyer of persons needs to know that the widow and the orphan have a Redeemer, a Protector of family rights. His name is the living God.

James 1:27

"Pure religion and undefiled before God and the Father is this, to visit the fatherless and widows in their affliction, and to keep himself unspotted from the world."

<u>Message</u>

My friend, some people go through religion or the external aspects of worship, with an unclean heart. James is confirming that the externals of religious activities are not acceptable to God unless accompanied by a holy life and loving service. Rites and rituals have never been an adequate substitute for service and sacrifice. Pure religion does not merely give material goods for the relief of the distressed, it also oversees the needs. Orphans and widows were among the most unprotected and needy classes in ancient societies. So my friend, remember the fatherless; they need to be encouraged with a word from the LORD. Just let them know that their Heavenly Father loves and cares about them and He cares about you as well.

Day 8:

Seek

TODAY'S SCRIPTURES:
Deuteronomy 4:28-31
I Chronicles 28:9
Isaiah 55:6
Matthew 7:7-11
Colossians 3:1-4

Definition of Seek
Try to find, look for, hunt, search for, try to get, attempt to make a search.

Deuteronomy 4:28-31

"And there ye shall serve gods, the work of men's hands, wood and stone, which neither see, nor hear, nor eat, nor smell. But if from thence thou shalt seek the LORD thy God thou shalt find him, if thou seek him with all thy heart and with all thy soul. When thou art in tribulation and all these things are come upon thee, even in the latter days, if thou turn to the LORD thy God, and shalt be obedient unto his voice. For the LORD thy God is a merciful God. He will not forsake thee neither destroy thee, nor forget the covenant of thy fathers which he sware unto them."

Message

My friend, we just read in the word of God that we are to seek the LORD like never before. The LORD was telling the children of Israel through Moses, to seek the living God and not the Gods that are made out of wood. Those words even apply to us today. Seek the Living God and you will find Him and He will open up your understanding and will direct you to His Son Jesus Christ.

I Chronicles 28:9

"And thou, Solomon my son, know thou the God of thy father, and serve him with a perfect heart and with a willing mind: for the LORD searcheth all hearts, and understandeth all the imaginations of the thoughts: if thou seek him, he will be found of thee; but if thou forsake him, he will cast thee off for ever."

Message

My friend, again this word is not just for Solomon but it is also for you. You are reading this book, you have the riches of Solomon, you have everything your heart desires when it comes to material things, but deep down in your soul you still are yearning for something and you can't explain it. You have talked with your wealthy friends and you still can't figure it out. It is not by chance you are reading this book, but it was ordained of God for you to purchase this book. My friend, you must acknowledge that you are a sinner and repent of your sins and ask Jesus Christ to come into your heart. When you do this Christ is going to reveal Himself to you through the Holy Spirit. True service of God is more than rational and intellectual. It requires a commitment of the emotions as well. This was precisely where Solomon failed. Even though he had great wisdom he allowed his heart to turn aside from God. Remember, loyalty of heart is essential for faithful effective service. Seek the LORD!

Isaiah 55:6

"Seek ye the LORD while he may be found, call ye upon him while he is near:"

Message

To seek the LORD is to seek His word my friend. Read the word of God and see what it has to say pertaining to your life. I don't care what kind of situation you find yourself in, the word of God is there to give you answers to direct you to what you need to do in every situation in your life. Seek the LORD in His word.

Matthew 7:7-11

"Ask and it shall be given you; seek and ye shall find, knock and it shall be opened unto you. For everyone that asketh receiveth, and he that seeketh findeth: and to him that knocketh it shall be opened. Or what man is there of you, whom if his son ask bread, will give him a stone? Or if he ask a fish will he give him a serpent? If ye then, being evil, know how to give good gifts unto children, how much more shall your father which is in heaven give good things to them that ask him?"

Message

My friend, the word of God is telling us that everything we need has been promised to us. The blessing and the provisions of God are available to every one of His children.

Colossians 3:1-4

"If ye then be risen with Christ, seek those things which are above, where Christ sitteth on the right hand of God. Set your affection on things above not on things on the earth. For ye are dead, and your life is hid with Christ in God. When Christ, who is our life shall appear, then shall ye also appear with him in glory."

Message

My friends, don't just concentrate on temporal observances, but concentrate on the eternal realities of heaven. We as Christians must continually discipline ourselves to focus on eternal realities, instead of the temporal realities of this earth. Our lives can no longer be dictated by this world, but they must be hidden with Christ. My Christian friend, we must seek The LORD!

Day 9:

TODAY'S SCRIPTURES:
Psalm 4:4
Psalm 8:2
Psalm 46:10
Psalm 65:7
Psalm 76:8
Mark 4:39

Still

Definition of Still

To stay in the same position or at rest, without noise, quiet, tranquil, making no sound, silent.

Psalm 4:4

"Stand in awe, and sin not: commune with your own heart upon your bed, and be still. Selah."

Message

My friend, the LORD wants you to be still, commune with your heart and trust God. There are some things you are trying to work out or talk out, but just be still. God is working it out!

Psalm 8:2

"Out of the mouth of babes and sucklings hast thou ordained strength because of thine enemies, that thou mightest still the enemy and the avenger."

Message

My friend, "He's got the whole world in His Hands." That's the song that came to me while I was writing this verse. The LORD has the whole wide world in His hands, and He will make our enemies be still, just like HE did for the children of Israel when it was time for them to cross the Red Sea. My friend, God is causing your enemies to be still so just continue to trust and praise Him cause He is working for you. Be still and keep your mouth closed.

Psalm 46:10

"Be still and know that I am God; I will be exalted among the heathen, I will be exalted in the earth."

Message

My friend just be still. The call for stillness before the LORD is not a preparation for worship, but for impending judgment. My friend, God is the judge. God will be exalted. And all the earth will bow before Him. Be still. This trial that you are going through, God is judge and will have the last word and He will be exalted. Be Still!

Psalm 65:7

"Which stilleth the noise of the seas, the noise of their waves, and the tumult of the people."

Message

My friend, we serve an awesome God, and we serve Him through His Son Jesus Christ, a God who made the seas and quiets the noise of the sea and the waves. Friend, that's the kind of God I serve and I pray that you serve Him as well. I pray that you have repented of your sins and have asked Jesus Christ to come into your heart, so that you will believe and have confidence in Him.. Dear friend, before I accepted Christ in my life I used to wonder if God was really real and if He was concerned about me. But since I have accepted Christ in my life and as I continue to live for Him, God becomes more and more real to me and I know that He is concerned about me. I know He is working thing out for me so that He will be glorified.

Psalm 76:8

"Thou didst cause judgment to be heard from heaven; the earth feared, and was still."

Message

My friend, in God's victories over the enemies of His people, word of God's glory and justice spread to the entire world. The wrath of men became praise to God because any anger against God was utterly futile. A person's futile hostility to God will only result in a demonstration of God's power and a subsequent glorification of His name. Again my dear friend, when God tells you to be still, you can see through His word that He is going to execute judgment.   So just be still and watch God!

Psalm 83:1

"Keep not thou silence, O God: hold not thy peace and be not still, O God."

<u>Message</u>

My friend, David was asking God not to keep silent. He wanted God to act. He believed and we also believe that God as the Holy One would destroy all evil. Unfortunately, we fail to see that God's delay in judgment was, and still is, an expression of His mercy. So friend, just be still and keep your mouth shut; I am not just talking to you, I am talking to myself as well. There are times when God wants to work on our behalf and HE can't because we are too busy interfering.

Mark 4:39

"And he arose and rebuked the wind and said unto the sea, Peace, be still. And the wind ceased, and there was a great calm."

<u>Message</u>

First of all, Jesus was asleep. That right there shows his true humanity. He was fully human and needed food and rest just as all people. Jesus' command over the wind and the sea demonstrates His full and complete deity. Only God the Creator can calm wind and sea.

Day 10:

Milk

TODAY'S SCRIPTURES:
Isaiah 55:1
I Corinthians 3:2
Hebrews 5:12,13,14
I Peter 2:2

Definition of Milk

The whitish liquid secreted by the mammary glands of female mammals for the nourishment of their young.

Isaiah 55:1

"Ho, everyone that thirsteth, come ye to the waters, and he that hath no money: come ye buy, and eat yea come buy wine and milk without money and without price."

Message

My friend, in this scripture milk is a symbol of complete satisfaction. Not only does God's salvation supply what is necessary for life, but it also provides that which brings joy.

The portion of scripture that states, "he that hath no money: come ye buy," expresses that salvation cannot be bought, but is a free gift for those who desire it. Romans 6:23 says, "For the wages of sin is death, but the gift of God is eternal life through Jesus Christ our LORD." Friend, salvation is free through Jesus Christ, so repent of your sins.

I Corinthians 3:2

"I have fed you with milk and not with meat: for hither to ye were not able to bear it, neither yet now are ye able."

<u>Message</u>

My friend, Paul did not expect the Corinthians to be mature in Christ at the time of their conversion. He knew that it was pleasing to God for the Corinthians to place their faith in Christ; therefore, they were justified. They had been united with Him and His death on the Cross and the Spirit of God had come to live in them (Romans 6:3-5). They were considered righteous before God because of Jesus' righteousness. Thus, when Paul first established the church at Corinth, he taught them as new converts; as those who were justified. Yet, he expected them to grow in their faith and become sanctified. The behavior of the Christians in Corinth should have begun to line up with their righteous position in Christ. Friend, an immature Christian naturally lacks many Christian traits, but a mature Christian is able to distinguish between good and evil (Hebrews 5:14).

Hebrews 5:12-14

"For when for the time ye ought to be teachers, ye have need that one teach you again which be the first principles of the oracles of God: and are become such as have need of milk, and not of strong meat. For everyone that useth milk is unskillful in the word of righteousness: for he is a babe. But strong meat belongeth to them that are of full age, even those who by reason of use have their senses exercised to discern both good and evil."

<u>Message</u>

My friend, all believers ought to be teachers; not in the formal sense, but in the sense that those who have been taught, ought to impart to others what they have learned through the gifts God has given them. Friend, maturity comes through practice. As we practice righteousness, we will have less difficulty determining good from evil. The scripture uses the term "babe" to describe the spiritually immature. Babies have little discernment or self-discipline. They must be constantly told no. Mature believers are able to know right from wrong and to control their sinful appetites. My dear friend, those who make a habit of obeying the message of righteousness are mature in the faith and are able to distinguish good and evil.

I Peter 2:2

"As newborn babes, desire the sincere milk of the word, that ye may grow there by."

<u>Message</u>

My friend, desire does not mean to merely want something, but rather to long for something with all of ones being, that you may grow. The purpose of studying God's truth is not only to learn more, but also to become mature in the faith. My dear sweet friend, those who seek to grow into Christ-like maturity need to consider it carefully. Jesus provides for those who seek His help. All we need to do is ask.

Day 11:

TODAY'S SCRIPTURES:
John 2:11
John 6:26
John 9:16
John 11:47
Acts 2:22
Acts 19:11
I Corinthians 12:10

Miracles

Definition of Miracles

A wonderful happening that is contrary to, or independent of the known laws of nature, and is therefore ascribed to God or some supernatural being or power.

John 2:11

"This beginning of miracles did Jesus in Cana of Galilee and manifested forth his glory; and his disciples believed on him."

Message

My friend, in the Gospel of John, the miracles of Jesus are called signs. These miracles confirm that Jesus is Messiah. Friend, there are seven signs in John which are an organizing

73

principle of this Gospel. The sign signified Christ's glory, which is His deity. When He transformed water into wine He demonstrated His creative power. He did in a moment what is ordinarily done in weeks or in months. The conscious water glowed when it saw its Maker; it had no choice but to surrender to Jesus because of His authority.

John 6:26

"Jesus answered them and said Verily Verily, I say unto you, Ye seek me, not because ye saw the miracles, but because ye did eat of the loaves and were filled."

<u>Message</u>

My friend, Jesus rebuked their motives. He stated that although the people had seen the signs, they had not accepted them for what they were (proof of His true Messiahship). They were only interested in the physical. Friend, are you only interested in things that Christ can give or are you interested in what He has done for you? Christ died so that we can have life and have it more abundantly, and not only life abundantly my friend, but life eternally. Ask yourself what does Christ mean to you?

John 9:16

"Therefore said some of the Pharisees, This man is not of God because he keepeth not the sabbath day. Others said, how can a man that is a sinner do such miracles? And there was a division among them."

Message

My friend, the Pharisees could not believe that Jesus was from God because He healed on the Sabbath, thereby breaking the oral traditions that had grown up around the Law. But those who fairly evaluated Jesus' miraculous signs came to the conclusion that He was from God.

John 11:47

"Then gathered the chief priests and the Pharisees a council, and said, What do we? For this man doeth many miracles."

Message

My friend, the real concern of the Jewish leaders is seen here. They were not as upset at Jesus' supposed blasphemy as they were about losing their positions of authority. At times that same spirit is on some of our church leaders today, especially when God is using that so called "pew member" through signs and wonders. My dear friend, I am here to tell you; however God wants to use you through His Son Jesus Christ you need to tell Him YES!!! Let God deal with them. You are going to stand alone when you face God so be encouraged and do whatever God tells you to do, and say whatever He tells you to say.

Acts 2:22

"Ye men of Israel, hear these words' Jesus of Nazareth, a

man approved of God among you by miracles and wonders and signs which God did by him in the midst of you, as ye yourselves also know."

Message

My friend, Jesus Christ was God's provision for the judgment of sin, yet it was our sinfulness that made His death necessary. In other words it was both the sinfulness of humanity and God's plan to save humanity that put Jesus to death on the Cross. God exercises sovereign control over all events, even the death of His Son. Yet at the same time, people are still responsible for their own sinful actions.

Acts 19:11

"And God wrought special miracles by the hands of Paul."

Message

My friend, God confirmed Paul's apostolic authority by performing miracles through him. In the book of Hebrews the writer helps us to understand why miracles were accomplished through the apostles. The miracles verified that the apostles represented God and that the gospel they preached was from Heaven.

I Corinthians 12:10

"To another the working of miracles to another prophecy to another discerning of spirits to another the interpretation of tongues."

<u>Message</u>

My friend, we serve an awesome God. God works in believers to benefit the entire body, not just the individual Christian. The Christian is a vehicle through which God works toward the up-building and unity of the entire body. Once when I was living in Seattle, a friend of mine was moving into a new apartment but her furniture was too big to go up the stairs because of the wall. She tried and tried to move the furniture. Then we touched and agreed in prayer that God would shift the wall so the furniture could be moved. God worked a miracle and shifted the wall and she was able to get the furniture up the stairs.

Day 12:

Stand

TODAY'S SCRIPTURES:
Exodus 14:13-14
Psalms 94:16
Romans 11:20

Definition of Stand
Take or keep a certain position, remain the same, resist destruction, remain in a certain course or direction.

Exodus 14:13-14

"And Moses said unto the people, Fear ye not stand still and see the salvation of the LORD, which he will shew to you today: for the Egyptians whom ye have seen today ye shall see them again no more forever. The LORD shall fight for you and ye shall hold your peace."

Message

My friend, in this account in the Bible the Children of

Israel were under great pressure squeezed between the waters before them and the armies of Pharaoh behind them. God provided the way of escape; the people were to go forward not to go back and not to give up. My dear friend, you may be going through some situations now in your life, but I am here to tell you that the LORD says 'Stand Still!' He is going to bring you out. Just listen for His direction and do whatever He tells you to do.

Psalms 94:16

"Who will rise up for me against the evildoers? or who will stand up for me against the workers of iniquity."

<u>Message</u>

My friend, the LORD alone is our sure defense for the believer.

Romans 11:20

"Well because of unbelief they were broken off and thou standest by faith . Be not high minded, but fear."

<u>Message</u>

My friend, if it had not been for the grace of God, Gentiles would never have been grafted into the life of God, which the Jews enjoyed. The New Testament believer must not assume that they are better than Jews because they were cut off for their unbelief. Just think about it like this; it is much easier to put natural branches back on than to graft different branches in their place. So my friend, we therefore must rest totally on the grace of God for our salvation. Again, the Jews were broken off because of unbelief and we as Gentiles stand by faith. But Paul goes on to warn that the Gentiles should not be haughty, but fear standing before God based on faith. Feelings of superiority are out of place.

I Corinthians 16:13

"Watch ye, stand fast in the faith, quit you like men, be strong."

Message

My friend, Paul's exhortation to stand fast in faith is especially important as seen in the Corinthians' susceptibility to false teaching. He was emphasizing to be mature and do everything with love.

Day 13:

TODAY'S SCRIPTURES:
Psalms 37:3-5
Psalms 118: 8-9
Psalms 125:1-2
Psalms 144:2
Isaiah 12:2
Isaiah 50:10

Trust

Definition of Trust

Confidence or faith in a person or thing, to have confidence or faith in, believe, to expect, to depend on.

Psalms 37:3-5

"Trust in the LORD and do good so shall thou dwell in the land, and verily thou shalt be fed. Delight thyself also in the LORD and he shall give thee the desires of thine heart. Commit thy way unto the LORD trust also in him; and he shall bring it to pass."

Message

My friend, the theme of this psalm is patience, a

renewed sense of dependence on the LORD, and a new sense of pleasure in knowing Him. When Christians have desires that spring from the LORD, the LORD will surely fulfill those desires.

Psalms 118: 8-9

"It is better to trust in the LORD than to put confidence in man. It is better to trust in the LORD than to put confidence in princes."

<u>Message</u>

My friend, if our trust is in the LORD's strength we do not have to fear the reprisals of our enemies. Relying on other people is part of living, but our ultimate trust can only be placed in the LORD God. Friend, even powerful leaders are limited by their own mortality. Trust God!

Psalms 125:1-2

"They that trust in the LORD shall be as mount Zion, which cannot be removed, but abideth forever. As the mountains are around about Jerusalem, so the LORD is round about his people from henceforth even forever."

<u>Message</u>

My friend, as said in the other songs of Zion, there is a deep belief in the invincibility of the city of Jerusalem because of the LORD's choice of Mount Zion. The psalmist proclaims that those who trust in the LORD will endure as the mountain that surrounds Jerusalem. The mountain provides protection for the city since any invading army would have to march through dangerous mountain paths. But we know the true protection comes from the LORD.

Psalms 144:2

"My goodness, and my fortress, my high tower and my deliverer; my shield, and he in whom I trust; who subdueth my people under me."

<u>Message</u>

My friend, David found in the LORD the protection and preparation he needed in times of battle, and you, my dear friend, are in a battle. So remember that God is in the battle with you.

Isaiah 12:2

"Behold God is my salvation, I will trust, and not be afraid for the LORD Jehovah is my strength and my song: He also is become my salvation."

<u>Message</u>

My friend, this scripture is based on the first psalm of redemption in Exodus 15:2 and also Psalms 118:14. Take some time to read and study the word of God today.

Isaiah 50:10

"Who is among you that feareth the LORD that obeyeth the voice of his servant that walketh in darkness and hath no light? Let him trust in the name of the LORD, and stay upon his God."

Message

My friend, the fear of the LORD and the reverence of God is the beginning of true wisdom. So continue to trust and fear God. He has great things in store for you.

Day 14:

TODAY'S SCRIPTURES:
Job 2:11
Psalms 23:4
Romans 15:4
I Corinthians 14:3
I Thessalonians 4:18
I Thessalonians 5:14

Comfort

Definition of Comfort
To ease the grief or sorrow of any that experiences trouble, freedom from pain.

Job 2:11

"Now when Job's three friends heard of all this evil that was come upon him, they came everyone from his own place; Eliphaz the Temanite, and Bildad the Shuhite, and Zophar the Naamathite: for they made an appointment together to come to mourn with him and to comfort him."

Message

My friend, I know many of you know the account

87

in the bible about Job. Job was a wealthy man and he lost everything that was dear to him in one day. He lost all of his cattle, children, etc. His friends came to comfort him and for seven days and nights they just sat and didn't say a word and listened to Job express himself. Later, when they began to share with Job, their words were not encouraging. They were words of blaming Job and saying that he was a sinner and that he must have sin to make these calamities come upon him. But the word of God said that Job was perfect and upright and one that feared God. So God allowed these things to happen to Job. My dear friend, you may be having a Job experience, but God is right there to comfort you. Some of your friends may act like Job's friends; blaming you for your calamity. But be encouraged, God is with you in this test, because it is just a test. This test is going to work out for your good just like it worked out for Job. At the end of Job's calamity, God restored everything that Job lost and more. Friend, read the account of Job and be comforted.

Psalms 23:4

"Yea though I walk through the valley of the shaddow of death, I will fear no evil; for thou art with me; thy rod and thy staff they comfort me."

<u>Message</u>

My friend, the Good Shepherd is with us through our most difficult and troubling situations. Just like the sheep are not alone, their shepherd is standing over them and guiding them into safety, so the LORD stands over us and protects us. My dear friend, I encourage you on today to get in the sheepfold, acknowledge that you are a sinner, repent of your sins and become a sheep. Our great shepherd Jesus Christ will lead you and guide you into green pastures.

Romans 15:4

"For whatsoever things were written aforetime were written for learning, that we through patience and comfort of the scriptures might have hope."

<u>Message</u>

My friend, through patience and the comfort of scriptures, believers learn that they have hope. If strong believers are patient with the weak, they will have hope of being rewarded. My dear friend, comfort someone on today.

I Corinthians 14:3

"But he that prophesieth speaketh unto men to edification, and exhortation, and comfort."

<u>Message</u>

My friend, being a Prophetess myself, I really appreciate the LORD using me to comfort His people with a word from Him. It really has been an awesome experience for me. God gave me the gift of prophecy and interpretation of tongues in

January 1978.

I Thessalonians 4:18

"Wherefore comfort one another with these words."

Message

My friend, the Thessalonians were talking about the second coming of Jesus Christ, indicating that it should be a constant comfort to us to think each day that the LORD may come.

I Thessalonians 5:14

"Now we exhort you, brethren warn them that are unruly, comfort the feeble minded, support the weak, be patient toward all men."

Message

My friend, the Thessalonians had to face the fact that some of them were not living as Christians should, but were unruly. They needed to be warned about their behavior. Some were fainting and needed comfort. As Christians, we should also uphold the weak and be patient toward all, recognizing that all Christians have faults. My dear friend, to be most effective in promoting positive change in people lives, believers should respond to individuals according to each ones particular needs.

Day 15:

TODAY'S SCRIPTURES:
Genesis 17:1
Leviticus 26: 12
Psalms 84:11
Romans 8:1-4
II Corinthians 5:7
Galatians 5:16
Ephesians 5:2

Walk

Definition of Walk

Go on foot, roam, go slowly, move or shake in a manner suggestive of walking, conduct oneself in a particular manner, behave, live (walking the ways of God), go over, on or through.

Genesis 17:1

"And when Abram was ninety years old and nine, the LORD appeared to Abram, and said unto him, I am the Almighty God, walk before me and be thou perfect."

Message

My friend, Abraham was ninety-nine years old when

God told him to walk before Him and be perfect. Prior to God telling him this, Abraham was 75 years old when he came to the land of Canaan. At 86, he became the father of Ishmael, then thirteen more years passed before Sarai conceived Isaac. God waited a long time before He fulfilled His promise to Abraham. As Enoch had walked with God, so now Abraham was commanded to walk before God. He was to conduct his life as an open display of faithfulness to the LORD. Abraham had integrity.

Leviticus 26:12

"And I will walk among you, and will be your God, and ye shall be my people."

Message

My friend, this is God's third promise; His presence in Israel's midst. He would actively walk among them, looking out for their welfare, helping and protecting them. Friend, this is the covenant by which God bound Himself to Israel and Israel to Him. The first promise and blessing that God promised them was the resources for abundant supplies of food including rain whenever it would be needed. The second promise and blessing was security or peace in the land. Neither animal nor human adversaries would be successful against Israel. My dear friend, God even protected them from lions and bears and any other dangerous animal. Any enemy that tried to attack Israel would be easily rerouted.

Psalms 84:11

"For the LORD God is a sun and shield: the LORD will give grace and glory: no good thing will he withhold from them that walk uprightly."

Message

My friend, this is the observation of a wise and righteous person. Time after time, God gives good gifts to His people, but God has also given us standards and principles that we are to live by.

Romans 8:1-4

"There is therefore now no condemnation to them which are in Christ Jesus, who walk not after the flesh, but after the Spirit. For the law of the Spirit of life in Christ Jesus hath made me free from the law of sin and death. For what the law could not do, in that it was weak through the flesh, God sending his own Son in the likeness of sinful flesh, and for sin, condemned sin in the flesh that the righteousness of the law might be fulfilled in us, who walk not after the flesh, but after the Spirit."

Message

My friend, in this scripture Paul depicts the freedom of living in the Spirit and having no condemnation in Christ. We are no longer under the sentence of anyone, but empowered by the spirit to live for Christ. The Holy Spirit energizes our renewed spirit, the God in us that has now been brought to life.

II Corinthians 5:7

"For we walk by faith, not by sight:"

Message

My friend, when we have the Holy Spirit we are no longer slaves to sin, but His children. So we receive all rights and privileges of Children of God. Christ is not physically present, so believers live by faith.

Galatians 5:16

"This I say then, walk in the Spirit and ye shall not fulfill the lust of the flesh."

Message

My friend, the flesh is the sinful properties that dwell in us. As a result of the fall, Satan works through the flesh to move us toward sin,whereas God works through our human spirit by His Holy Spirit to produce Christian virtues that please Him. So the only consistent way to overcome the sinful desires of our human nature (flesh) is to live step by step in the power of the Holy Spirit. Friend, as He works through our Spirit we have to walk each moment of faith in God's word. The inner conflict between the flesh and the Spirit is very real, but the Spirit's control assures absolute victory over the desires of our sinful nature.

Ephesians 5:2

"And walk in love as Christ also hath loved us, and hath given himself for us an offering and a sacrifice to God for a sweet smelling savour."

Message

My friend, in conclusion, we as believers are to follow the example of God's actions. He loved us when we were still His enemies. Therefore, as individuals who are seeking to be Christ-like, believers should demonstrate that type of self-sacrificial love.

Day 16:

TODAY'S SCRIPTURES:
Genesis 4:9-10
Leviticus 17:11
Matthew 26:27-28
Acts 20:28
Roman 3:25-26
Roman 5: 9-10
Ephesians 1:7

Blood

Definition of Blood

The liquid in the veins, arteries and capillaries of vertebrates, normally appearing to be red, but actually consisting of a fluid, pale-yellow plasma and semisolid red and white blood cells and platelets. Blood is circulated by the heart, carrying oxygen and digested food to all parts of the body and carrying away waste materials.

Genesis 4:9-10

"And the LORD said unto Cain where is Abel thy brother? And he said, I know not. Am I my brother's keeper? And he said, What hast thou done? The voice of thy brother's blood crieth unto me from the ground."

Message

My friend, that blood of Abel cries out until the blood of one more innocent than Abel is shed as well. Abel depicts the Savior Jesus who was killed by His countrymen, His brethren. They crucified Him and shed His innocent blood on the cross.

Leviticus 17:11

"For the life of the flesh is in the blood: and I have given it to you upon the altar to make an atonement for your souls: for it is the blood that maketh an atonement for the soul."

Message

My friend, the life of animals and humans is in the blood. If a creature loses its blood it loses its life. God appointed blood to have this power because it represents the life of the creature. The fact that there is blood flowing through the veins of animals and human beings is evidence of the vitality within them. A life may receive atonement only by the sacrifice of a life. In the book of Hebrews it is emphasized that the temporary nature of animal blood sacrifices required constant renewal. However, Jesus' one time sacrifice of Himself is effective eternally. Friend, it is the blood of Jesus that causes us to have salvation and eternal life. There is power in the blood of Jesus.

I want to share a testimony with you concerning the

Blood of Jesus. About a couple of months after I had been walking with Jesus, I was coming home from the store one evening just before dusk. I was walking through my apartment complex and a man came from behind me and grabbed my arms and tried to throw me down to the ground. I was so scared I didn't know what to do. Then the Holy Spirit bought back to my mind a testimony I heard in church about how a man had a knife to one of the saint's throats. The Holy Spirit told her to reach up and take his hand from around her neck and say the Blood of Jesus. She did and the man got afraid and told the woman that he was sorry and that he saw a whole group of Angels around her. So I begin to say, "Satan the LORD rebuke you and I plead the Blood of Jesus." When I pleaded the Blood of Jesus the man turned me loose and ran. There is power in the Blood of Jesus. When I meet you my friend, I will share another testimony with you concerning the Blood of Jesus.

Matthew 26:27-28

"And he took the cup and gave thanks, and gave it to them, saying, Drink ye all of it. For this is my blood of the new testament, which is shed for many for the remission of sins."

Message

My friend, the blood of the new covenant refers to the covenant that had been promised in the Old Testament. Jesus specifically said that His blood was shed for many for the remission of sins. The blessing of the New Covenant was to all in this age and it will yet be fulfilled for Israel in the future.

Acts 20:28

"Take heed therefore unto yourselves and to all the flock over the which the Holy Ghost hath made you overseers, to feed the church of God which he hath purchased with his own blood."

Message

My friend, the blood of the Son of God was shed for the sins of the church. This is part of Paul's farewell speech to the Elders at Ephesus. He was letting them know there are always two threats to the church; one from the outside and one from the inside. Unbelievers are a dangerous threat from the outside; the arrogant and self-serving are a threat from within.

Roman 3:25-26

"Whom God hath set forth to be a propitiation through faith in his blood to declare his righteousness for the remission of sins that are past through the forbearance of God. To declare, I say at this time his righteousness: that he might be just and justifier of him which believeth in Jesus."

Message

My friend, by His death Christ satisfied the justice of God. He paid the penalty of sin in full. Paul shares with us two reasons why the righteousness of God came through Christ's death. The first reason was to demonstrate that God Himself is righteous and did not judge the sins committed prior to the cross. The second reason is that God wanted to show that He is both righteous and at the same time, the One who can declare sinners righteous. Therefore, because of Christ's death, God does not compromise His holiness when He forgives a sinner.

Roman 5: 9-10

"Much more then, being now justified by his blood, we shall be saved from wrath through him. For if, when we were enemies, we were reconciled to God by the death of his Son, much more, being reconciled, we shall be saved by his life."

<u>Message</u>

My friend, If God loved us when we were helpless, ungodly enemies, how much more will He love us now that we are His children? Through the death of His Son and His blood, we have been justified, that is declared righteous and reconciled; meaning our state of alienation from God has been changed. Believers are no longer enemies of God, they are at peace with God and shall be saved. My dear friend, the point is that since God's love and the death of Christ have brought us justification, then as a result of that love we can also expect salvation from God's wrath. To experience this truth my friend, believers must fully cooperate with the process that is explained in Romans 6:1-14, 'shall we continue in sin…?'

Ephesians 1:17

"In whom we have redemption through his blood, the forgiveness of sins, according to the riches of his grace."

Message

My friend, first of all, redemption means brought back or ransomed. In ancient times, one could buy back a person who was sold into slavery. In the same way, Christ through His death brought us from our slavery of sin by His blood. The blood of Christ is the means by which our redemption comes. The Old Testament and the New Testament both clearly teach that there is no forgiveness, without the shedding of blood.

Day 17:

TODAY'S SCRIPTURES:
Genesis 40:14
Nehemiah 5:19
Jeremiah 29:11
Matthews 24:44
John 5:39
Ephesians 3:20
Philippians 4:8
I Peter 4:12

Definition of Think

To form a thought or idea in the mind, consider, intend or plan, expect, contemplate the matter, have an opinion.

Genesis 40:14

"But think on me when it shall be well with thee and shew kindness. I pray thee, unto me and make mention of me unto Pharaoh and bring me out of this house."

Message

My friend, Joseph asked the butler to remember him so that his case might be reviewed and he might be delivered from a false imprisonment. Joseph spoke of a binding obligation that his interpretation of the dream had placed upon the butler. Presumably the butler would recognize the unfairness of Joseph's condition, since he himself had been unfairly charged and badly treated as well.

Nehemiah 5:19

"Think upon me, my God, for good, according to all that I have done for this people."

Message

My friend, first of all, Nehemiah was Governor of Jerusalem. He wanted to please God. He was a man of dependence upon God. He knew that God would fight for him. He was always thinking about God and His people. Friend, every leader needs to read about Nehemiah. His project of rebuilding the wall of Jerusalem was never an end in itself. The ultimate objective was to revitalize the people of Israel and return them to their covenant with God. To that end, after the wall was completed, Nehemiah turned the city management over to the local government leaders. He did not create dependency on his own skills nor did he use the project to gain wealth or fame for himself. My dear friend, Nehemiah was a leader that served the people. That is what we are supposed to be, servants of the people and not ourselves.

Jeremiah 29:11

"For I know the thoughts that I think toward you, saith the LORD, thoughts of peace, and not of evil, to give you an expected end."

Message

My friend, The LORD places considerable emphasis on His unchangeable plan to bring peace and not evil and a future, a hope. God had not terminated His relationship with Judah and HE has not terminated His relationship with you. My dear friend, God loves you so much that He gave His only begotten Son so that you may have life and life more abundantly—eternal life. He is a God of promises and He will not break His promises. Friend, think on these things and know that God is always there for you. It doesn't matter when or where, God is always there.

Matthew 24:44

"Therefore be ye also ready: for in such an hour as ye think not the Son of man cometh."

Message

My friend, just like Noah was vigilant in preparing for the flood, so should people be alert in preparation for Christ's return.

John 5:39

"Search the scriptures, for in them ye think ye have eternal life and they are they which testify of me."

<u>Message</u>

My friend, the Jewish religious leaders of Jesus' day diligently searched the Old Testament scriptures, but did not see Jesus as the Messiah and did not believe in Him. There are also those today who master the scriptures, but do not allow the scriptures to master them. God doesn't promise to bless those who do Bible reading, but rather Bible heeding. Friend, their problem was not a lack of evidence, it was a lack of willingness to consider any evidence that would bring them to Christ.

Ephesians 3:20

"Now unto him that is able to do exceeding abundantly above all that we ask or think according to the power that worketh in us."

<u>Message</u>

My friend, God can do exceeding abundantly above anything we may ask. Neither God's love nor His power is limited by human imagination. Think my dear friend, think!

Philippians 4:8

"Finally my brethren whatsoever things are true, whatsoever

things are honest, whatsoever things are just, whatsoever things are pure, whatsoever things are lovely, whatsoever things are of good report; if there be any virture, and if there be any praise, think on these things."

Message

My friend, we as Christians can renew our minds so that we will not conform to the evil habits of this world.

I Peter 4:12

"Beloved think it not strange concerning the fiery trial which is to try you, as though some strange thing happened unto you."

Message

My friend, for Christians, the purpose of suffering is to prove their true character, to shed sin from man and to allow the pure nature of Christ to show itself. Christians should expect and prepare for suffering. My dear friend, some suffering that we experience is natural and must be expected. However, some suffering will come specifically from Christ and will have serious eternal consequences. This suffering will be directed toward both Christians and non-Christians, but the outcome for each group will be significantly different.

Day 18:

TODAY'S SCRIPTURES:
Psalms 95:6
Psalms 97:7
Psalms 99:5
Matthews 4:9
John 4:21-23
Philippians 3:3

Worship

Definition of Worship

(Shachah) To bow, to stoop, to bow down before someone as an act of submission or reverence, to fall or bow down when paying homage to God, to make oneself low, especially in the presence of God.

Psalms 95:6

"Come let us worship and bow down: let us kneel before the LORD our maker."

Message

My friend, this verse describes a physical posture of humility before the LORD. The Hebrew translation of the word worship means literally to prostrate oneself. My dear friend, when bowing down, kneeling, and worship occur together as in this verse, they amplify each other and call for a reflective, humble approach to God. Worship is joyful, but at other times worship may be quiet reverence of the Almighty.

Psalms 97:7

"Confounded be all they that serve graven images, that boast themselves of idols: worship him, all ye gods."

Message

My friend, the continuing practice of idolatry throughout world history is a grave offense against the LORD. Such behavior will ultimately end in shame and terror. Anything that serves as an object of worship will one day bow before the true God. My dear friend, in this day and time there is a whole lot of idolatry taking place; people are worshiping animals (cows), people, and statues. People worship money and cars. My friend, in the end we are all going to bow down to the true and living God.

Psalms 99: 5

"Exalt ye the LORD our God, and worship at his footstool; for he is holy."

Message

My friend, the footstool of the LORD is sometimes

said to be the earth. When the Israelites came to the temple in Jerusalem to worship, they pictured themselves as being at the feet of the Creator.

Matthew 4:9

"And saith unto him, All these things will I give thee, if thou wilt fall down and worship me."

Message

My friend, Christ rebuked the devil for asking for worship - a temptation to do exactly the opposite of what every Israelite was called upon to do. Satan was offering a crown without a cross. Jesus' experiences serve as a pattern in spiritual warfare today. Jesus resisted Satan than He defeated Satan with consistent meaningful use of the scripture. Satan has so many people under his influence and they are in the church today. Friend, Satan is offering them a crown without a cross. The cross stands for suffering.. Jesus suffered on the cross for our sins. They beat Him, spat on Him and pierced His side with a sword.

John 4:21-24

"Jesus saith unto her, Woman, believe me, the hour cometh, when ye shall neither in this mountain, nor yet at Jerusalem, worship the Father. Ye worship ye know not what: we know what we worship: for salvation is of the Jews. But the hour cometh, and now is, when the true worshipers shall worship the father in spirit and in truth: for the Father seeketh such to worship him. God is a spirit: and they that worship him must worship him in spirit and in truth."

Message

My friend, Christ reveals to the woman that where a person worships is unimportant. It is not limited to Mount Gerizim or Jerusalem. The Samaritans worshiped what they did not know; they had created their own religion. The Jews had divine guidelines for worship. The words 'Salvation is of the Jews' means that the Messiah would come from the Jewish people. My dear friend, God is not limited by time and space. When people are born of the Spirit, they can commune with God anywhere. Spirit is the opposite of what is material and earthly. Christ makes worship a matter of the heart. Truth is what is in harmony with the nature of God. It is the opposite of all that is false. My friend, the issue is not where a person worships, but how and who.

Philippians 3:3

"For we are the circumcision, which worship God in the spirit, and rejoice in Christ Jesus, and have no confidence in the flesh."

Message

My friend, Paul defines true circumcision as a matter of the heart and not of the flesh. Paul reveals three aspects of true circumcision and they are worshiping God in the spirit, rejoicing in Christ and placing no confidence in any human, honor or accomplishment as a means to reach God.

Day 19:

TODAY'S SCRIPTURES:
II Samuel 22:19
Psalms 18:17 18 19
Isaiah 48:2
Isaiah 50:10
Daniel 4:35

Stay

Definition of Stay
To continue to be as indicated, remain, stop, halt, pause, wait, delay, make a stand, put off, hold back.

II Samuel 22:19

"They prevented me in the day of my calamity: but the LORD was my stay."

Message

My friend, in this chapter David was thanking God for all the things that God had brought him through. God brought him through his pollution of a humble home and murder of

Uriah. Divine judgments overtook him in the denunciation by Nathan, the prophet and in the death of the babe during his son Absalom's rebellion. My dear friend, David was thanking God for all the calamity and his misfortune. Through it all, God still loved David and said he was a man after His own heart.

Psalms 18:17-19

"He delivered me from my strong enemy, and from them which hated me: for they were too strong for me. They prevented me in the day of my calamity: but the LORD was my stay. He brought me forth also into a large place; he delivered me, because he delighted in me."

<u>Message</u>

My friend, again God delivered his servant David from any power that might hold him. God is the LORD of all. My dear friend, God takes pleasure in those that serve Him.

Isaiah 48:2

"For they call themselves of the holy city, and stay themselves upon the God of Israel, The LORD of hosts is his name."

<u>Message</u>

My friend, in the holy city Jerusalem, the citizens of Jerusalem professed to lean on the God of Israel. The context is a reference to God's promises to Israel. My dear friend, God's purposes and promises have not failed.

Isaiah 50:10

"Who is among you that feareth the LORD, that obeyeth the voice of his servant, that walketh in darkness, and hath no light? Let him trust in the name of the LORD, and stay upon his God."

<u>Message</u>

My friend who fears the LORD; the fear of the LORD, which is the reverence or awe of God, is the beginning of true wisdom.

Daniel 4:35

"And all the inhabitants of the earth are reputed as nothing: and he doeth according to his will in the army of heaven, and among the inhabitants of the earth: and none can stay his hand or say unto him, what doest thou?"

<u>Message</u>

My friend, Nebuchadnezzar praises the Most High, recognizing that God lives forever and rules forever. My dear friend, the king unmistakably acknowledges Daniel's God as the Omnipotent, Eternal Sovereign of the Universe.

Day 20:

Servant

TODAY'S SCRIPTURES:
Deuteronomy 5:15
Psalms 116:16
Proverbs 17:2
Daniel 6:20
Malachi 1:6
Matthew 25:21
Matthew 25:30
John 13:16
Philippians 2:7

Definition of Servant

A person employed in a household, a person employed by a department or branch of government, a person devoted to any service. Ministers are called the servants of God.

Deuteronomy 5:15

"And remember that thou wast a servant in the land of Egypt and that the LORD thy God brought thee out thence through a mighty hand and by a stretched out arm, therefore the LORD thy God commanded thee to keep the sabbath day."

119

Message

My friend, the Israelites were to remember Israel's past oppression and celebrate their current freedom. Christians differ as to how this commandment relates to believers in Jesus Christ. The Sabbath was Saturday, the seventh day of the week. Christians generally worship God on Sunday, the first day of the week, because it was on a Sunday that the LORD rose from the dead. Christians follow the principles of this command. They dedicate time to the LORD by resting, by praising Him for His blessing and by remembering His saving acts written in the Bible.

Psalms 116:16

"O LORD truly I am thy servant; I am thy servant, and the son of thine handmaid; thou hast loosed my bonds."

Message

My friend, the psalmist declares that he is God's servant. As Jesus demonstrated in the Upper Room celebration of the Passover, every true follower of Christ must become a servant. Jesus the Son of God became a servant to His disciples and washed their feet, so every believer needs to serve others as well.

Proverb 17:2

"A wise servant shall have rule over a son that causeth shame and shall have part of the inheritance among the brethren."

Message

My friend, reversals of fortune could have happened if the wise servant was sufficiently skillful and the son and his brothers were undeserving. Much of the book of Genesis describes the rise of an unexpected younger son over his older brother. The two sons are referring to Esau and Jacob. The first-born would have preeminence, but this time God chose to bless the younger. Esau sold his birthright, so he lost his benefits to his younger brother Jacob.

Daniel 6:20

"And when he came to the den, he cried with a lamentable voice unto Daniel: and the king spake and said to Daniel, O Daniel, servant of the living God, is thy God, whom thou servest continually, able to deliver thee from the lions?"

Message

My friend, to ensure that the den remained closed and that no effort could be made either by the king or his officials to intervene the lid of the den was impressed with the royal seal and with the seals of the king's lords. The lid of the den could not be removed without breaking the seals. Yet, through all of that, God delivered Daniel, and my dear friend, God is going to deliver you as well. So rest my friend, God is going to bring deliverance to you today.

Matthew 25:21

"His LORD said unto him well done thou good and faithful servant thou hast been faithful over a few things, I will make thee ruler over many things: enter thou into the joy of thy LORD."

Message

My friend, the faithful and wise servant will be given larger responsibilities in the LORD'S Kingdom.

Matthew 25:30

"And cast ye the unprofitable servant into outer darkness: there shall be weeping and gnashing of teeth."

Message

My friend, the unprofitable servant is one who fails to be faithful to the tasks given by the master. Friend, this servant will not share in the rewards.

John 13:16

"Verily, Verily, I say unto you. The servant is not greater than his LORD; neither he that is sent greater than he that sent him."

Message

My friend, first all, washing feet was not a Jewish

ordinance. Jesus was dealing with attitudes. He was teaching them that there was only one who was willing to do the thing that everyone knew needed to be done, but nobody did because they were too interested in being served rather than serving. My dear friend, Christ is not suggesting that a ritual foot washing be established, but that His humble example of love in self-sacrificing service and forgiveness be followed. The person who practices these things will be blessed.

Philippians 2:7-8

"But made himself of no reputation and took upon him the form of a servant and was made in the likeness of men. And being found in fashion as a man, he humbled himself, and became obedient unto death, even the death of the cross."

Message

My friend, Christ continued in the very nature of God, but added to Himself the nature of a servant, the lowest status on the social ladder; the exact opposite of the term LORD, a title by which all will one day recognize the risen and exalted Christ. Therefore, it is truly amazing that the God who created the universe and who rules over all creation, would choose to add to His person the nature of a servant. Friend, in reality, Christ was a man possessing all the essential aspects of a human being, although unlike others, He was sinless.

Day 21:

Time

TODAY'S SCRIPTURES:
Psalms 37:19
Psalms 41:1
Psalms 53:6
Ecclesiastes 3: 1
Ecclesiastes 9:11
Hosea 10:12
Saint Matthew 26:18
Saint Luke 19:44
John 7:6
Roman 13:11

Definition of Time

All the days there have been or ever will be; the past, present and future, lifetime, years of living, a particular season, date or span of calendar system of measuring.

Psalms 37:19

"They shall not be ashamed in the evil time: and in the days of famine they shall be satisfied."

Message

My friend, God knows our circumstances and provides for us; God knows how long we will live and will sustain us to the end. God also knows that our days on earth are only the beginning of our days with Him in eternity.

Psalms 41:1

"Blessed is he that considereth the poor: the LORD will deliver him in time of trouble."

Message

My friend, the poor refers not only to those who do not have enough money, but also to those who suffer illness or misfortune through no fault of their own. For such persons, God is Defender, Deliverer and Sustainer. My dear friend, when I read this scripture I was encouraged because I am going through some things in my own personal life, and I can hear people in the spirit talking and discussing my problems and situations. I hear them saying, "Since she is always talking about God this, and God that, let us see how God is with her." Sometimes people will even withdraw their support from you. But friend, I am like you; let's see what God is going to do. I believe that God is with me because I serve an unlimited God.

Psalms 56:3

"What time I am afraid, I will trust in thee."

Message

My friend, I will have confidence even in this, the time of distress. My dear friend, I am in a time of distress now in my life. I can't do anything but trust God, and you my friend, must trust as well because He is going to bring you out of that situation.

Ecclesiastes 3:1

"To everything there is a season and a time to every purpose under the heaven:"

Message

My friend, this scripture speaks with eloquence of the role of time in the life of the believer. The preacher is not teaching that everything has an opportune time according to who chooses one action or the other. My dear friend, he teaches that all events are in the hand of God, who makes everything happen in the time He judges appropriate.

Ecclesiastes 9:11

"I returned, and saw under the sun, that the race is not to the swift nor the battle to the strong, neither yet bread to wise, not yet riches to men of understanding, nor yet favour to men of skill; but time and chance happeneth to them all."

Message

My friend, we would like to think that the best always win, that the deserving are always rewarded. But our experience shows that these expectations are not always realized; not by the swift, strong, wise men of understanding;

men of skill. These five assets were enjoyed by individuals. While some planned and counted on their assets, it was God in the end that determined their lot. Who was swifter than Asahel (II Samuel 2:22,23), stronger than Samson (Judges 16: 9), wiser than Solomon (I King 11:1-25) more discerning than Ahithophel (II Samuel 16:23; 17:5-14) or more learned than Moses (Exodus 2:11-15; Acts 7:22)? Yet, each met his limit and was encountered by God.

Hosea 10:12

"Sow to yourselves in righteousness, reap in mercy; break up your fallow ground: for it is time to seek the LORD, till he come and rain righteousness upon you."

<u>Message</u>

My friend, Hosea calls the people to repentance, reminding them that a decision could not be postponed, and that God's blessings could still be restored. My dear friend, plowing and planting are necessary preliminary steps for growing a crop, which eventually sprouts when the rain falls in season. In the same way, repentance would set the stage for restored blessing, which God would eventually rain down on His people.

Matthew 26:18

"And he said, Go into the city to such a man, and say unto to him, The Master saith, My time is at hand; I will keep the passover at thy house with my disciples."

Message

My friend, this was the first day of the Feast of the Unleavened Bread. It was also the day of the Passover and the LORD was talking to Peter and John.

Luke 19:44

"And shall lay thee even with the ground and thy children within thee; and they shall not leave in thee one stone upon another, because thou knewest not the time of thy visitation."

Message

My friend, Jesus gave the reason for the judgment; they did not recognize the time of God's coming Messiah.

John 7:6

"Then Jesus said unto them, my time is not yet come: but your time is always ready."

Message

My friend, earlier Jesus told His mother that His hour had not yet come. He also told His brothers that the time for manifesting Himself to the world had not yet come. My dear friend, Jesus mentioned on several occasions that the time for

Him to be publicly manifested on the cross was in the future.

Romans 13:11

"And that, knowing the time, that now it is high time to awake out of sleep: for now is our salvation nearer than when we believed."

<u>Message</u>

My dear friend, sleeping believers are dormant; they are simply existing and not living. Salvation refers to the future, when believers will be saved from the presence of sin. My dear friend, salvation here speaks of the imminent return of Christ.

Day 22:

Study

TODAY'S SCRIPTURES:
Ecclesiastes 12:12
I Thessalonians 4:11
II Timothy 2:15

Definition of Study

Effort to learn by reading, thinking or observing, a careful examination, investigation, earnest effort, or the object of endeavor or effort, deep thought, try to learn, consider with care, think, plan.

Ecclesiastes 12:12

"And further, by these, my son, be admonished: of making many books there is no end; and much study is a weariness of the flesh."

Message

My friend, many other books may weary their readers.

131

However, I think careful study of Ecclesiastes will have the opposite effect as it instructs, warns, and admonishes its reader. My dear friend, Ecclesiastes is one of the most misunderstood books in the bible. Christians have tended to either ignore the message of the book or regard it as the testimony of a man living apart from God. This is unfortunate, for the book asks relevant, searching questions about the meaning of life. It declares the utter futility of an existence without God. Like all scriptures, the book of Ecclesiastes benefits and edifies God's people.

I Thessalonians 4:11

"And that ye study to be quiet, and to do your own business and to work your own business and to work with your own hands, as we commanded you."

<u>Message</u>

My friend, Paul exhorted the Thessalonian believers to lead a quiet life, not referring to a lack of activity, but rather to an inner quietness and peace befitting the Christian faith. My dear friend, we should not be busybodies, but should mind our own business. Usually people who are busy running other people's affairs do not run their own affairs well. We, as Christians, should be dedicated and productive workers so that we might bring honor to Christ's name. Paul was a tent maker. What is your profession? Study to be quiet and take care of your own business.

II Timothy 2:15

"Study to shew thyself approved unto God, a workman that needeth not be ashamed rightly dividing the word of truth."

<u>Message</u>

My friend, I encourage you the way Paul encouraged Timothy; to handle the word of truth in a straight way; like a road that goes straight to its goal, without being turned aside by useless debates.

Day 23:

TODAY'S SCRIPTURES:
Psalms 41:11
Proverb 25:21, 22
Proverb 27:6
Saint Matthew 5:43-44
Galatians 4:16

Enemy

Definition of Enemy
One hostile to another, one who hates and desires or attempts the injury of another, a foe, an adversary, as an enemy of or to a person, an enemy to truth or to falsehood.

Psalms 41:11

"By this I know that thou favourest me, because mine enemy doth not triumph over me."

Message

My friend, the failure of David's enemy to destroy his life was an indicator of God's pleasure in David. David was a righteous person who was suffering in this psalm, but he was not an unrepentant sinner. I believe his ultimate hope was to glorify and praise God in His presence forever.

Proverb 25:21-22

"If thine enemy be hungry give him bread to eat; and if he be thirsty give him water to drink: For thou shalt heap coals of fire upon his head, and the LORD shall reward thee."

<u>Message</u>

My friend, the idea is that an act of kindness to your enemy may cause him or her to feel ashamed. This is just one way to overcome evil with good.

Proverb 27:6

"Faithful are the wounds of a friend; but the kisses of an enemy are deceitful."

<u>Message</u>

My friend, correction given in love by a friend is better than insincere acts of affection (Psalms 141:5).

Matthew 5:43-44

"Ye have heard that it hath been said, Thou shalt love thy neighbor, and hate thine enemy. But I say unto you, Love your enemies, bless them that curse you, do good to them that hate you, and pray for them which despitefully use you, and persecute you;"

Message

My friend, the phrase 'hate your enemy' is not found in Moses writings. This was a principle drawn by the scribes and Pharisees. Vengeance belongs to God partly because human vengeance is often carried out too zealously, but God's vengeance is entirely just. My dear friend, you shall love your neighbor as yourself. Jesus identified this as one of only two commandments that if kept would fulfill all the law.

Galatians 4:16

"Am I therefore become your enemy, because I tell you the truth?"

Message

My friend, a person with pure motives and real friendship does not always say things that are pleasant to hear. Paul was telling the Galatians the truth. As a result of Paul's honesty, he was labeled as their enemy. Sometimes the truth hurts, but a faithful friend would courageously confront another. Paul also told the Galatians to follow his example because he had abandoned the ceremonial rules and regulations connected with Judaism, so that he could freely preach the gospel of Christ to the Jews and Gentiles alike in the cities of Galatia. He hoped that they too would not hinder the gospel of Christ with laws and regulations.

Day 24:

TODAY'S SCRIPTURES:
Psalms 4:8
Psalms 29:11
Isaiah 9:6
Isaiah 26:3
Isaiah 45:7
Isaiah 48:22
Saint Matthew 10:13
Roman 14:17-19
Colossians 3:15
Galatians 5:22
Philippians 4;7

Peace

Definition of Peace
A state of physical or mental tranquility, calm, serenity, the absence of war, the state of harmony between people.

Psalms 4:8

"I will both lay down in peace, and sleep; for thou LORD, only makest me dwell in safety."

Message

My friend, the peace that God gives is far from a relaxation technique. It is a peace that enables an anxious person to lie down and sleep. Friend, even when torn by physical and

139

emotional pain, a person may still have a restful sleep.

Psalms 29:11

"The LORD will give strength unto his people; the LORD will bless his people with peace."

Message

My friend, the LORD will give strength since He is the true God. There is none other. My dear friend, He can empower His people. Only God can give us peace.

Isaiah: 9:6

"For unto us a child is born, unto us a son is given: and the government shall be upon his shoulder: and his name shall be called Wonderful, Counselor, The mighty God, The everlasting Father, The Prince of Peace."

Message

My friend, we serve the Prince of Peace. There is so much peace in the Son of God. When you serve the Son of God, Jesus Christ, you can go to the Prince of Peace for peace whenever you have troubles and problems. Isn't God good?,

Isaiah 26: 3

"Thou wilt keep him in perfect peace, whose mind is stayed on thee: because he trusted in thee."

Message

My friend, if you trust God you will be in peace; in perfect peace, my dear friend.

Isaiah 45:7

"I form the light and create darkness: I make peace, and create evil: I the LORD do all these things."

Message

In the Middle East, people commonly believed that the fertility of the earth and the maintenance of the social order depended on the king's right relationship with a deity. Therefore, because Cyrus was anointed by the true God, Heaven would shower its blessing on the earth. My dear friend, we know no other person or object that can compare to the power of our living Creator. HE is sovereign over everything, both good and evil.

Isaiah 48:22

"There is no peace, saith the LORD, unto the wicked"

Message

My friend, the wicked are the people that refuse to accept Jesus Christ as their Savior. So when they have problems and situations they have no one to call on. They may call on their manmade gods; however, they have no peace in

THERE IS A WORD FROM THE LORD

their heart or in their mind. Friend, if you are a born again Christian, you know who we call on when we have problems. We call on the Prince of Peace and He gives us peace in the midst of our situation.

Matthew 10:13

"And if the house be worthy, let your peace come upon it: but if it be not worthy, let your peace return to you."

<u>Message</u>

My friend, to greet a household was to pronounce a blessing on it. An example of this would be, peace unto you. Messengers were to assume the best of their hosts when they arrived; however, if the home proved to be unworthy, the occupants rejected the message. Friend, just as the apostles were to pronounce blessings, today, we as Christians, have that same authority to pronounce a blessing upon a home.

Romans 14:17

"For the kingdom of God is not meat and drink, but righteousness, and peace, and joy in the Holy Ghost."

<u>Message</u>

My friend, the Kingdom of God does not consist of external things like food, but in spiritual realities like righteousness in action and thought and peace that seeks harmony and joy, which come from the Holy Spirit. My dear friend, those who understand the spiritual realities of the Kingdom, will not choose the brief joy of satisfying selfish desires, over the spiritual joy of putting aside those desires for the sake of others. Friend, our service to Christ is rooted in righteousness, peace and joy.

Galatians 5:22-23

"But the fruit of the Spirit is love, joy, peace, longsuffering, gentleness, goodness, faith, meekness, temperance: against such there is no law."

Message

My friend, peace is a work done by the Holy Spirit Himself in the believer's life. It is well for the Christian to remember that without Christ and His Spirit you can do nothing. There is no peace without Christ being in your life.

Philippians 4:7

"And the peace of God which passeth all understanding shall keep your hearts and minds through Christ Jesus."

Message

My friend, the mind is in a battle zone and needs to be protected by a military guard, which is the Holy Spirit. Just as the purpose of such a guard in wartime situations is either to prevent a hostile invasion or to keep the inhabitants of a besieged town from escaping, so the peace of God operates in the same way; to protect the mind from external, corrupting influences and to keep the mind focused on God's truth.

Colossians 3:15

"And let the peace of God rule in your hearts, to the which also ye are called in one body; and be thankful."

<u>Message</u>

My dear friend, when we completely surrender to God's will, our whole being is unified in obedience to Him. Christ's sacrifice and reconciling work makes this surrender possible.

Day 25:

Praise

TODAY'S SCRIPTURES:
Psalms 22:25
Psalms 33:1
Psalms 34:1
Psalms 50:23
Psalms 66:2
Psalms 67:3
Psalms 69:34
Psalms 71:6
Psalms 148:3

Definition of Praise

Saying that a thing or person is good, words that tell the worth or value of a thing or person, commendation, words or song worshiping God.

Psalms 22:25

"My praise shall be of thee in thy great congregation: I will pay my vows before them that fear him."

Message

My friend, when I read this scripture, I reflect back to December 1977, when I first started to go to church and gave my life to the LORD. I was sitting on the pew watching the

145

saints praise the LORD. As I watched the saints praise the LORD, I said to myself that I needed to do what they were doing. So, my dear friend, I started to say thank you Jesus, I started to say hallelujah and glory, glory! It was simply wonderful. As I continued to praise the LORD, it was the best feeling I have ever experienced. I was just a new babe in Christ and to me it was a high without a hangover. Praise Him my friend.

Psalms 33:1

"Rejoice in the LORD ye righteous: for praise is comely for the upright."

<u>Message</u>

My friend, praise is something that naturally comes over you when you become born again. God sees the praises from believers as a beautiful sacrifice. Throughout Psalms, many instruments were employed to praise the name of the LORD. Friend, praise is always directed to the One who deserves all praise, glory, and honor, the LORD Almighty.

Psalms 34:1

"I will bless the LORD at all times: his praise shall continually be in my mouth."

<u>Message</u>

My friend, I know since I accepted Christ in my life

over 30 years ago, there has not been a day that I didn't praise the LORD. It's like a natural thing you do every day. My dear friend, you can always find something to praise God for. Even through your trials and tribulations, you should praise God. You have to be able to praise God during the good times and the going-through times. Friend, praise is natural for a born again believer, it is just as natural as breathing air.

Psalms 50:23

"Whoso offereth praise glorifieth me: and to Him that ordereth his conversation aright will I shew the salvation of God."

Message

My friend, in the climatic revelation of the coming judgment in this psalm, the LORD offers an opportunity to repent and receive forgiveness. My dear friend, this is an indicator of His grace. The LORD wants to save; His warnings are another expression of His mercy. Friend, if you have not acknowledged that you are a sinner and repented of your sins, now is the time to do so. Repent and ask Christ to come into your heart. You will be amazed by the things that Christ will start to do in your life when you tell Him Yes.

Psalms 66:2

"Sing forth the honor of his name; make His praise glorious."

Message

My friend, the LORD is pleased with music that praises HIS glorious name. The LORD'S name describes His character; so honoring God's name is honoring God. My friend, begin to Praise God for what He has already done and for what HE'S going to do in your life.

Psalms 67:3

"Let the people praise thee O God: let all the people praise thee."

Message

My friend, God's desire is for all people to praise Him, for He is the Creator and the Provider. My dear friend, this should also be the desire of God's people, all of HIS people. Just like people begin to yell and praise players when they make a touchdown in football or a foul shot in basketball, so friend, you need to praise the LORD. When you are at home, go somewhere private and began to praise the LORD, and He will come in the midst and talk with you.

Psalms 69:34

"Let the heaven and the earth praise him, the seas and everything that moveth therein."

Message

My friend, this is a powerful verse. The LORD is

telling us again to let everything praise Him, the heaven and the earth, the seas and everything that moveth therein. That included everything that is in the water, the fish, shrimp, and alligator etc., everything my friend. We serve a powerful God. He made everything and He wants us all to praise Him and give Him thanks and be thankful. Praise Ye The LORD!

Psalms 71:6

"By thee have I been holden up from the womb: thou art he that took me out of my mother's bowels; My praise shall continually of thee."

Message

My friend, God is a wonder. David declares that the work of God in his life made him a special sign to the people, similar to the great miracles of God through Moses and Aaron in Egypt.

Psalms 148:3

"Praise ye him, sun and moon all ye stars of light."

Message

My friend, the entire universe is called to boast of the wonder of God.

Day 26:

Fire

TODAY'S SCRIPTURES:
Exodus 3:2
Exodus 40:38
I King 19:12
Psalms 66:12
Isaiah 43:2
Saint Matthew 3:11
Saint Mark 9:44-45
Acts 2:3-4
Jude 22-23
Revelation 20:11-15

Definition of Fire
Consuming flame, heat and light caused by something burning.

Exodus 3:2

"And the angel of the LORD appeared unto him in a flame of fire out of the midst of a bush: and he looked and behold, the bush burned with fire and the bush was not consumed."

Message

My friend, this was an extraordinary sight, since the bush was not consumed. My dear friend, when I was mediating, this is what the LORD gave me to share on today.

Thus saith the LORD; "He will begin to have visitation with some pastors because they have gotten discouraged." Pastors, the LORD loves you and He is with you.

Exodus 40:38

"For the cloud of the LORD was upon the tabernacle by day, and the fire was on it by night, in the sight of all the house of Israel, throughout all their journeys."

Message

My friend, the book of Exodus ends with the image of our wonderful God, hovering protectively over His people; and my friend, He is even over us today with all His splendor and power.

I Kings 19:12

"And after the earthquake a fire; but the LORD was not in the fire: and after the fire a still small voice."

Message

My friend, God is not just a God of the spectacular, but God can be experienced in a still small voice, the sound of gentle stillness. My dear friend, that's the way I heard the audible voice of the LORD when He spoke to me. It was a quiet, still voice and He said to me, "This day, I have given you the gift of prophecy and interpretation of tongues." That was over 30 years ago.

Psalms 66:12

"Thou hast caused men to ride over our heads; we went through fire and through water: but thou broughtest us out into a wealthy place."

Message

My friend, God has seen us go through the fiery trials and through the water of life. But you are now on your way to your wealthy place in God. In the wealthy place, you have more than enough. So remember to share the wealth and testify of His goodness.

Isaiah 43:2

"When thou passest through the waters, I will be with thee; and through the rivers; they shall not overflow thee; when thou walkest through the fire thou shalt not be burned; neither shall the flame kindle upon thee."

Message

My friend, passing through the waters is an allusion to the crossing of the Red Sea and the Jordan River. Walking through the fire is a metaphor for protection in danger. Consider the LORD's protection of Shadrach, Meshach, and Abednego in the fiery furnace. God bought them out of the furnace and He will bring you out as well.

Mark 9:44-45

"Where their worm dieth not, and the fire is not quenched. And if thy foot offend thee, cut it off: it is better for thee to enter halt into life, than having two feet to be cast into hell, into the fire that never shall be quenched."

<u>Message</u>

My friend, hell is real. I had a visitation about hell. It was like a vision and a dream; it was so real to me. I was newly saved and I did something wrong. I went to bed, and it was as if I went to sleep; however, I dreamed that I got caught up in the rapture. Then, all of a sudden, I started to fall back down into darkness. I could hear the weeping and the gnashing of teeth, just like the scriptures speak of in Matthew 8:12. Friend, I quickly repented and got myself together. The LORD was letting me know that hell was real and that I really needed to say yes to Him, and I did.

Acts 2:3-4

"And there appeared unto them cloven tongues like as of fire, and it sat upon each of them. And they were all filled with The Holy Ghost, and began to speak with other tongues as the Spirit gave them utterance."

<u>Message</u>

My friend, in the scriptures, fire was often symbolic of

the presence of God. When I first spoke in tongues, I was in my bedroom praying to the LORD. I was telling Him that people at the church said that I needed to receive the gift of the Holy Ghost and that when I did; I would speak in another language. Well friend, while I was praying, I began to speak in another tongue. I put my hand in my mouth, trying to stop it, but I kept on speaking in this language. It was a glorious experience and the presence of God was in my bedroom.

Jude 22-23

"And of some have compassion, making a difference: And others save with fear, pulling them out of the fire; hating even the garment spotted by the flesh."

Message

My friend, we have certain obligations to other believers. We need to show mercy to those in any kind of spiritual or physical need. My dear friend, we need to use discernment in helping our brothers and sisters in the church. Some will require tender care and patience to help them to grow in Christ, while sometimes, we may need to use drastic actions to rescue them from the temptation of sin. Remember, in rescuing our fellow believers, there is always the need to use wisdom and caution to prevent getting caught up in the sin that caused them to fall. Paul reminds us and I am reminding you, to consider yourself lest you also be tempted (Galatians 6:1).

Revelations 20:9-10

"And they went up on the breadth of the earth, and compassed the camp of the saints about, and the beloved city: and fire came down from God out of heaven, and devoured them. And the devil that deceived them was cast into the lake of fire and brimstone, where the beast and the false prophet are and shall be tormented day and night forever and ever."

Message

My friend, this scripture refers to the coming time when the LORD will put down the final rebellion. The devil will join the beast and the false prophet in torment forever in the lake of fire.

Revelations 20:11

"And I saw a great white throne, and him that sat on it, from whose face the earth and the heaven fled away; and there was found no place for them."

Message

My friend, the great white throne is a picture of God's holy rule and judgment.

Revelations 20:12-15

"And I saw the dead small and great stand before God: and the book was opened which is the book of life: and the dead were judged out of those things which were written in the books according to their works. And the sea gave up the dead which where in it; and death and hell delivered up the dead which were in them and they were judged every man according to their works. And death and hell were cast into the lake of fire. This is the second death. And whosoever was not found written in the book of life was cast into the lake of fire."

Message

My friend, both believers and unbelievers will stand before the great white throne. Christians will experience the first resurrection and not endure the great white throne judgment. The opening of the book will lead to eternal sentencing, you will be judged acceptable based on your work. Unbelievers, humanity will be judged according to its works will be cast into the lake of fire. Only God's elect names are written in the book of life, these are the born again Christians who will escape the lake of fire.

Day 27:

TODAY'S SCRIPTURES:
Genesis 46:34
I Samuel 17:40
Psalms 23:1
Isaiah 40:11
Ezekiel 34:5
John 10:14-16
Hebrews 13:20
I Peter 5:4

Shepherd

Definition of Shepherd
Person who takes care of sheep, person who cares for and protects, a spiritual guide, pastor, take care of, guide, direct.

Genesis 46:34

"That ye shall say, Thy servants trade hath been about cattle from our youth even until now, both we, and also our fathers: that ye may dwell in the land of Goshen: for every shepherd is an abomination unto the Egyptians."

Message

My friend, Joseph was faced with a bit of a problem: how to introduce his long lost family to Pharaoh. His brothers and father were shepherds and ranchers. Those occupations were an abomination to the Egyptians. Joseph told his brothers to boldly claim their skills, rather than downplay their occupations. Pharaoh respected Joseph and requested that his family take care of his livestock. Friend, the assignment matched the skills and they prospered; and you too shall prosper, if you will do what God has tasked you to do.

I Samuel 17:40

"And he took his staff in his hand, and chose him five smooth stones out of the brook, and put them in a shepherd's bag which he had, even in a scrip; and his sling was in his hand: and he drew near to the Philistine."

Message

A sling was the typical equipment of a shepherd. And with a stone, David killed Goliath.

Psalms 23:1

"The LORD is my shepherd I shall not want."

Message

My friend, David's uses for God came from his own life and experience, since David had been a shepherd in his youth.

Isaiah 40:11

"He shall feed his flock like a shepherd: he shall gather the lambs with his arm, and carry them in his bosom, and shall gently lead those that are with young."

Message

My friend, in the ancient Middle East, the ideal king was often depicted as a shepherd.

Ezekiel 34:5

"And they were scattered, because there is no shepherd: and they became meat to all the beasts of the field when they were scattered."

Message

My friend, having leaders who seek to be served, rather than to serve, is like having no leader at all. The people of Israel were like sheep without a shepherd. The Israelites wandered aimlessly, and they were easily attacked. Friend, my prayer for you is that you are under one of the shepherds who are after God's own heart.

John 10:14-16

"I am the good shepherd, and know my sheep, and am known of mine. As the father knoweth me, even so know I the father; and I lay down my life for the sheep. And other sheep I have, which are not of this fold: them also I must bring, and they shall hear my voice; and there shall be one fold, and one shepherd."

<u>Message</u>

My friend, a good shepherd has an intimate knowledge of his sheep. The interaction between Christ and His followers is something like the fellowship between a Father and His Son. Friend, the other sheep were the Gentiles, and to the Jews they were called heathens. For the Jews, the Gentiles' salvation would form one spiritual body.

I Peter 5:4

"And when the chief Shepherd shall appear, ye shall receive a crown of glory that fadeth not away."

<u>Message</u>

My friend, Jesus is the Chief Shepherd and the Good Shepherd. God guarantees that those ministers who serve Him faithfully in accordance with His word will receive an eternal reward in Christ's coming Kingdom.

Day 28:

TODAY'S SCRIPTURES:
Genesis 3:10
Exodus 5:2
II Samuel 22:14
I Kings 19:12
Ezekiel 43:2
Saint Matthew 17:5
John 12: 28-29
Acts 9:34
Revelation 3:20

Voice

Definition of Voice
Sound made through the mouth, especially by people speaking, singing, shouting etc. The human voice is produced in the larynx.

Genesis 3:10
"And he said I heard the voice in the garden, and I was afraid, because I was naked and I hid myself."

Message

When Adam heard God's voice, he was afraid and guilty because he knew he had disobeyed God. My dear friend, please obey when you hear the voice of the LORD speak to you. Sometimes you can miss the blessing of God because of disobeying His voice. People, deliverance is in your hands; so please friend, obey the voice of God.

Exodus 5:2

"And Pharaoh said, who is the LORD that I should obey his voice to let Israel go? I know not the LORD, neither will I let Israel go."

<u>Message</u>

My friend, the spirit of Pharaoh is still in our midst today. So many of God's people are in bondage because the Pharaoh of leadership will not let God's people go. They will not encourage God's people to do the things that God has put in their heart to do. My dear friend, man is building up his kingdom on earth, so that he can drown out the voice of God in your life, and the people of God are listening more to the voice of leadership and fear than they are listening to HIS voice. Friend, train yourself to listen to and obey God's voice.

II Samuel 22:14

"The LORD thundered from heaven, and the most high uttered His voice."

<u>Message</u>

In this scripture, David was praising the LORD because God had delivered him from the hand of all his enemies. My dear friend, if God can deliver David from all his enemies, HE can deliver you from yours. I am praying, and you need to pray, that God delivers you from all of your enemies. We may not even know who all of our enemies are, but God does.

I King 19:12-13

"And after the earthquake a fire; but the LORD was not in the fire: and after the fire a still small voice. And it was so, when Elijah heard it, that he wrapped his face in his mantle, and went out, and stood in the entering in of the cave. And behold, there came a voice unto him, and said, What doest thou here, Elijah?"

Message

My friend, Elijah learned that God is not just a God of the spectacular, but a God of gentle stillness. For His voice was still and quiet.

Ezekiel 43:2

"And behold the glory of the God of Israel, came from the way of the east and his voice was like a noise of many waters and the earth shined with his glory."

Message

My friend, Ezekiel is sharing his experience concerning the LORD'S voice. Think about what kind of experience you have had with the LORD and share it with someone; and they will truly be blessed.

Matthew 17:5

"While he yet spoke, behold, a bright cloud overshadowed them: and behold a voice out of the cloud, which said, This is my beloved Son, in whom I am well pleased; hear him."

Message

My friend, this event recorded in Matthew, was a witness to Christ's divinity. In the midst of Peter talking and telling Jesus what they needed to do concerning the three tabernacles, Christ's transfiguration took place.

John 12:28-29

"Father, glorify thy name. Then came there a voice from heaven, saying, I have both glorified it, and will glorify it again. The people therefore, that stood by, and heard it, said that it thundered: others said, an angel spake to him."

Message

My friend, I believe Christ's ultimate desire was to glorify His Father's name, and now, my dear friend, the Father answers from heaven; that His Name has been glorified because of the obedient ministry of His Son; and that it will be glorified again through His death, burial and resurrection.

John 10:4

"And when he putteth forth his own sheep, he goeth before them, and the sheep follow him: for they know his voice."

Message

My friend, do you know the voice of the LORD when He speaks to you? God can speak in many ways, but we must have an ear to hear what thus saith the LORD. Friend, ask God to give you an ear to hear Him when He speaks to you.

Acts 9:3-4

"And as he journeyed, he came near Damascus, and suddenly there shined round about him a light from heaven. And he fell to the earth and heard a voice saying unto him Saul, Saul, why persecutest thou me?"

Message

My friend, the light that shone around Saul was brighter than the sun. It was so penetrating that Saul fell to the ground and so did everyone that was with him. My dear friend, Saul had been persecuting the church, so when he heard a voice, but did not see anyone, he was speechless. Are you hearing the voice of God today? He is speaking to you today, so obey Him.

Revelation 3:20

"Behold, I stand at the door, and knock: if any man hear my voice, and open the door, I will come in to him, and will sup with him, and he with me."

Message

My friend, Jesus is seeking entrance into His own church for the purpose of renewed fellowship. This passage is often interpreted as Christ knocking at the door of an individual unbeliever's heart, though the context makes that unlikely.

Day 29:

TODAY'S SCRIPTURES:
Exodus 1:7
Psalms 36:8
Isaiah 55:7
John 10:10
Ephesians 3:20

Abundantly

Definition of Abundantly

Existing in great or overflowing quantity, very plentiful, well supplied.

Exodus 1:7

"And the children of Israel were fruitful, and increased abundantly, and multiplied, and waxed exceeding mighty, and the land was filled with them."

Message

God multiplied a small family of twelve sons and one daughter into a nation that would conquer Canaan. My dear friend, God's hand in the incredible growth of Israel's family,

169

was a miracle.

Psalms 36:8

"They shall be abundantly satisfied with the fatness of thy house; and thou shalt make them drink of the river of thy pleasures."

<u>Message</u>

My friend, the wicked are never satisfied, but the one who trusts in the LORD can find ample satisfaction.

Isaiah 55:7

"Let the wicked forsake his way, and the unrighteous man his thoughts: and let him return unto the LORD, and he will have mercy upon him; and to our God, for he will abundantly pardon."

<u>Message</u>

My friend, we serve a kind God that loves His creation, and when we forsake our wicked ways and even our unrighteous thoughts, His word tells us that He will abundantly pardon. My dear friend, receive God's pardon through His Son Jesus Christ.

John 10:10

"The thief cometh not but for to steal, and to kill, and to destroy: I am come that they might have life, and that they might have it more abundantly."

Message

My friend, the thief takes the life that the sheep give it. My dear friend, an abundant life includes: salvation, nourishment, healing, peace, love, and much more. This is a quality life with Christ here on earth, and also an eternal life that will be complete and perfect.

Ephesians 3:20

"Now unto him that is able to do exceeding abundantly above all that we ask or think, according to the power that worketh in us,"

Message

My friend, neither God's love nor His power is limited by human imagination. Our God can do anything!

Day 30:

TODAY'S SCRIPTURES:
Leviticus 19:17-18
Deuteronomy 6:5
Psalms 116:1
Psalms 145:20
Matthew 5:43,44,45
John 14:15
John 14:22,23
John 15:12
I Peter 1:8

Love

Definition of Love

A warm and tender liking, deep feelings of fondness and friendship, great affection or devotion, the kindly feeling or benevolence of God for His creatures, or the reverent devotion due from mankind to God. Love is also an unselfish loyal and benevolent concern for the good of another: as (1): the fatherly concern of God for humankind (2): brotherly concern for others.

Leviticus 19:17-18

"Thou shalt not hate thy brother in thine heart: thou shalt in any wise rebuke thy neighbour and not suffer sin upon him. Thou shalt not avenge nor bear any grudge against the children

173

of thy people, but thou shalt love thy neighbor as thyself: I am
the LORD."

Message

The commands of God always flow out of His
character, and we, as Christians, should strive to have that
same character. My friends, Christians are growing in grace,
but sometimes we get out of character. We are not perfect.
My dear friend, don't hate your brother in your heart. Jesus
addressed this principal in the Sermon on the Mount. The
way to avoid hatred and bitterness is to confront the person.
Rebuke your neighbor. This involves resolving the issues
face to face. My friend, vengeance belongs to God, because
human vengeance often is carried out too zealously. But God's
vengeance is entirely just. The phrase 'bear any grudge', means
to actively keep a grudge alive with an eye towards vengeance.
You shall love your neighbor as yourself. Jesus identified this
as one of only two commandments that if kept, would fulfill
all of the law.

Psalms 116:1

"I love the LORD because he hath heard my voice, and my
supplications."

Message

My friend, I love the LORD and I am so glad he hears
my supplications. My dear friend, God looks from His place

of glory to meet the needs of His people. I love the LORD.

Psalms 145:20

"The LORD preserveth all them that love him: but all the wicked will he destroy."

Message

My friend, continue to love the LORD, because He will preserve you, no matter how old you are.

Matthew 5:43-45

"Ye have heard that it hath been said, Thou shalt love thy neighbor, and hate thine enemy. But I say unto you, Love your enemies, bless them that curse you, do good to them that hate you, and pray for them which despitefully use you, and persecute you; That ye may be the children of your Father which is in heaven: for he maketh his sun to rise on the evil and on the good, and sendeth rain on the just and on the unjust."

Message

My friend, when it rains, it rains on everyone that goes out in it. When the sun is shining, it will shine on you if you are out in it. God is good, and He cares about all of His creation. He loves us so much that He gave us His only begotten Son. My dear friend, hating your enemy is not found in Moses' writing. This was a principle drawn by the Scribes and Pharisees. Friend, we are to be like our Heavenly Father who loves without discrimination.

John 14:15
"If ye love me, keep my commandments."

Message
My friend, love is not just sentimental emotionalism, it is obedience to the commandments of God.

John 14:22-23
"Judas saith unto him, not Iscariot, LORD how is it that thou wilt manifest thyself unto us, and not unto the world?
Jesus answered and said unto him, If a man love me he will keep my words: and my Father will love him, and we will come unto him, and make our abode with him."

Message
My friend, if a believer loves and obeys the LORD, he or she will experience fellowship with God. My dear friend, the fellowship is sweet and it is real. You can have fellowship everyday with the LORD, just love and obey.

John 15:12
"This is my commandment, That ye love one another, as I have loved you."

Message

My friend, the command to love was new because Jesus gave it a new standard. Moses said to love your neighbor as yourself, but Jesus said the new standard was, 'as I have loved you.' Therefore, Jesus gave His disciples the example of love that they were to follow. My dear friend, unbelievers recognize Jesus' disciples, not by their doctrinal distinctions, nor by dramatic miracles, nor even by their love for the lost. They recognize His disciples by their deeds of love for one another. The early church caught hold of this fantastic principal of incendiary love. Friend, the mark of a Christian is love. It is the greatest apologetic for Christ.

I Peter 1:8

"Whom having not seen, ye love; in whom, though now ye see him not, yet believing, ye rejoice with joy unspeakable and full of glory:"

Message

My friend, the phrase 'having not seen,' is explaining that only a few believers had the privilege of walking and talking with Jesus when He was on the earth. Most of us have shared the experience of Paul, who never knew Jesus personally or saw Him physically, but loved and believed in Christ anyway. My dear friend, I am grateful to the LORD for opening my eyes and letting me see how real He is.

Day 31:

Pray

TODAY'S SCRIPTURES:
Genesis 20:7
I Samuel 7:5
Psalm 55:17
Isaiah 45:20
Saint Matthew 5:44
Saint Matthew 26:41
Saint Luke 6:12
Saint Luke 18:1
I Thessalonians 5:17
I Timothy 2:8

Definition of Pray

Speaking to God in worship, entering into spiritual communion with God, offering worship, making earnest requests to God, imploring, beseeching.

Genesis 20:7

"Now therefore restore the man his wife; for he is a prophet, and he shall pray for thee, and thou shalt live: and if thou restore her not, know thou that thou shalt surely die, thou, and all that are thine."

Message

My friend, in my studies, this is the first use of the term

179

prophet in the bible that indicates more than a relationship to God—but the ability to speak for Him. Abraham's relationship to God was the basis for God's command that Sarah be restored to her husband. God warned the king about the wrong he was getting ready to commit because of Abraham's deception about Sarah. But in the end, it worked out for the good, because King Abimelech was a pagan king. When he asked Abraham why he deceived him regarding Sarah, Abraham explains why. The people learned about the power of the Lord God because they were able to witness it. God closed all of the women's wombs; therefore, they were not able to bring forth any children. However, Sarah was able to conceive while she and Abraham were living in Gerar. This information is revealed in Genesis 21:1-2. Abraham wasn't the only one to protect himself by concealing his relationship to his wife. His son Isaac did the same thing with his wife Rebekah, which is found in Genesis 26.

I Samuel 7:5

"And Samuel said, Gather all Israel to Mizpah, and I will pray for you unto the LORD."

Message

In this account, the Children of Israel were serving strange gods and Samuel was letting them know that if they would serve the living God, HE would deliver them out of the hand of the Philistines. They repented, God forgave them and HE delivered them out of the hands of the Philistines. Samuel earnestly prayed for the Children of Israel and cried out to GOD. The Children of Israel would not want to go into battle unless Samuel was praying for victory. When I read this account, I could not help but to reflect on how earnestly Samuel's mother, Hannah, prayed for him. She prayed and asked God for a son. Now, her son was grown, and he was praying for a nation of people to be delivered from their enemies, the Philistines. My friend, as the old folks say, "The apple doesn't fall far from the tree." Samuel was a praying man and God answered his prayers. In the two scriptures I have shared with you, the son Isaac did the same thing as his father in Genesis, but the LORD brought him out and blessed him and his household. Samuel was a praying man.

Psalms 55:17

"Evening, and morning, and at noon, will I pray, and cry aloud: and he shall hear my voice."

<u>Message</u>

My friend, our praying to God in the name of Jesus is not in vain because God hears our prayers just like he heard David's prayer in this Psalm. David just had to remind himself of the great acts of deliverance that God had done on his behalf in the past, and the work that God would continue to do in the future. We too must remind ourselves of God's faithfulness in our life, and how He answered our prayers, especially when we are in distress.. He may not come when you want Him to, but He will always be there right on time.

Isaiah 45:20

"Assemble yourselves and come; draw near together, ye that are escaped of the nations: they have no knowledge that set up the wood of their graven image, and pray unto a god that cannot save."

<u>Message</u>

The Israelites were shocked that the Lord had appointed a foreign pagan to carry out His will—a Persian King by the name of Cyrus. This king was put over His people. The Lord had called him as a shepherd and anointed him to carry out His will. So, when King Cyrus called the Children of Israel to assemble together, he was letting them know that the God you serve is the God that can save and not the god that cannot save—a god made of wood and graven image. God was letting them know that He was the same God who made a promise to Abraham and that He was making that promise to them also.

Matthew 5:44

"But I say unto you, Love your enemies, bless them that curse you, do good to them that hate you, and pray for them which despitefully use you, and persecute you;"

Message

God is so good. He knew what we were going to experience as members of the Kingdom of God; therefore, He gave us these beatitudes. My friend, we have to have the right attitude and ask God to help us to have the right attitude when we go through these experiences. Remember my friend, prayer changes things. So, we have to pray that God changes us, because if we don't, we will go through these challenges.

Luke 6:12

"And it came to pass in those days, that he went out into a mountain to pray, and continued all night in prayer to God."

Message

This scripture provides an example of how Jesus spent time with God, the Father, before an important event occurred in his life. Other examples of Jesus praying to God are found in Luke 3:21 and Luke 22:41-44. My friend, as Christians, we ought to follow the examples of those who went before us. We have to earnestly seek God in prayer when we are about to go through a major event in our lives.

Matthew 26:41

"Watch and pray, that you enter not into temptation: the spirit indeed is willing, but the flesh is weak."

Message

In this account, the disciples needed to stay awake and pray because they were about to be tested. Every child of God needs supernatural empowerment because the flesh is truly weak. We also have to remember what Romans 8:3-4 teaches us. We have to continually seek out the things of the Spirit. One way to ensure that we are following after the Spirit is to pray. When the soldier came to get Jesus that night, the disciples met their test, but they were not ready.

Luke 18:1

"And he spoke a parable unto them to this end, that men ought always to pray, and not to faint;"

Message

Just like the persistent widow that Jesus spoke of, God does not begrudgingly answer prayers; however, insensitive judges will. The judge responded to the continual request of the widow just as God our Father will certainly respond to the persistent prayer of the believers.

I Thessalonians 5:17

"Pray without ceasing."

Message

My friend, praying without ceasing doesn't mean to

pray constantly, it means being consistently in prayer. You have to communicate with God each and every day so that you will know what His will is at all times.

1Timothy 2:8

"I will therefore that men pray everywhere, lifting up holy hands, without wrath and doubting."

Message

In this passage, the men refer to those who were involved in leading public worship. Public worship is not restricted to elders or those with specific gifts. Prayer is one of the essential features of Christian worship.

— FINAL MESSAGE —

 $\mathcal{M}$ y friend, I pray that you have been blessed and encouraged by reading these messages that God has given me. I hope that you hide this encouragement in your heart and reflect on the goodness of God each and every day. Remember that there is nothing too difficult for God and that this race is not given to the swift, but to he or she that endures until the end. Rejoice in the fact that you are still standing. Praise God for delivering you out of your distress. It doesn't matter what it looks like with the natural eyes, you have to see the heart of the matter. God is a God who looks at the heart, and so we must also look at the heart. Celebrate the conclusion of the matter because it has already been done. Remember, Jesus said that we would do what He did and greater, so why are we concerned? Just rest in the LORD and wait patiently. God already knows what you need and how you need it. He has already made a way for it to come to pass, even before you were born.

The bottom line is that as long as you stay with God and allow Him to order your steps, you win. If you're feeling a little down, remember that the joy of the LORD is your strength. Most of all, know that you have been bought with a price. Through Jesus' great sacrifice, we now have a lively hope. Yesterday is gone, but what about today? What do you want God to do in your life today? How are you going to glorify God today? Seek God in all things. It will work out for your good just because you love Him and were called according to His purpose. It is not enough to say that you love God, but it must be done in deed and in word. Reading the Word is a good thing. Now it is time to live the Word and let it live in you. No matter what, trust God! Men will let you down, family will disappoint you, friends will come and go, but God always was and always will be right where you need Him to be, and He will supply your every need.

— ABOUT THE AUTHOR —

$\mathcal{P}$rophetess Stephanie Moore was born in Norfolk, Virginia. She is the daughter of the Late Marvin L. Daniels and the late Pearlie E. Daniels. She graduated from Norfolk City Schools and then went on to pursue a Bachelor's degree at Norfolk State University. Prophetess Moore is currently attending Amridge University, where she is majoring in Human Resources. She has been a faithful and diligent servant to the call and work of the Lord for many years. Prophetess Moore is currently a member of The Experience Church (*It Can't Be Explained, It Can Only Be Experienced!*) in Suffolk, Virginia under the leadership of Pastor John A. Moore, III.

Prophetess Moore received the prophetic gift approximately 34 years ago during a New Year's Revival in 1978. Evangelist Deborah Thomas was praying for the people at the revival. When Evangelist Thomas came to pray for Prophetess Moore, who was Sister Moore at the time, she asked her what she wanted. Prophetess Moore asked for a triple portion of the Holy Ghost. Prophetess

Moore began to speak in tongues and praise GOD; she went home speaking in tongues. When she woke up in the morning, Prophetess Moore heard a wind and then she heard a quiet and still voice; the LORD's voice sounded like a many of waters, just like it says in Ezekiel 43:2. The LORD said, "This day I have given you the gift of prophecy and interpretation of tongues."

Prophetess Moore recently retired from Hampton City Schools, where she served as an Instructional Assistant for twenty two years. She is the proud grandmother of Amorae and Assani and mother of daughter Darlisha Moore, son Pastor John A. Moore, III, and his wife Kenya. She writes about her experiences hearing from the LORD in hopes of inspiring others to listen and obey GOD.

Made in the USA
Middletown, DE
19 July 2020